Be Present At Our Table, Lord

Be present at our table, Lord;
Be here and everywhere adored;
Abide with us and grant that we
May feast in Paradise with thee.
Amen.

(Sung to the tune of Doxology)

CANADA
A ROCHA
Environmental Stewardship

River Tree Press
19353 16th Avenue
Surrey, BC
V3Z 9V2
www.arocha.ca

Copyright © 2014 by River Tree Press
This edition, 2015

ISBN 978-0-9940956-0-2

Printed in United States of America

Edited and collated with love
by Pamela Soo
Fall 2013

Copyedited by Shai Kroeker & Leah Kostamo

Contents

Creator, Sustainer, Redeemer, thank you for the gift of another day and for the chance to be together. Thank you for providing our daily bread, reminding us of our day-by-day dependence on your creation. For your presence in our lives we thank you. May we learn from our own lives, from each other, and from your presence among us.
Amen.

Prayer from *Food and Faith*, edited and compiled by Michael Schut

Introduction

Ding! Ding! Ding! Ding! Ding! Five long bells ring. It's 12.15pm.

Dingdingdingdingdingdingdingdingdingding! It's 12.30pm.
It's time to gather for lunch in the Main House Community Room at Brooksdale.

We stand around the tables, eagerly awaiting the chef(s) on duty to announce what's on the menu and pick a song to bless the meal. We enjoy the good food before us, the fellowship around the table and the love we share in Jesus.

In myriad ways, food is a big part of the A Rocha Canada story. It weaves through the fabric of our daily work across the country - community living, hospitality, environmental education, sustainable agriculture and conservation projects.

For a while now, an idea of our cookbook has been floating around.A collection of kitchen staples and food stories that have represented the flavours of A Rocha Canada, both in our kitchen and beyond. This is our first little endeavour to do just that!

We humbly present to you our very own A Rocha Canada cookbook! It has been joyfully filled with favourite recipes as well as a sprinkle of reflections and a drizzle of quotes. We hope these will be both inspirational and educational, and give you glimpses of life and work at Brooksdale Environmental Centre.

Our big dream for this cookbook is to grow it into a shared community project across our regional centres that will bless her readers richly - whether staff or volunteers, local or international, new or seasoned cooks.

There are two spiritual dangers in not owning a farm.
One is the danger of supposing that breakfast comes from the grocery,
and the other that heat comes from the furnace.

Aldo Leopold

While staying at A Rocha, I've had to learn how to use a lot of interesting vegetables that I'd never come across before and new ways to prepare vegetables that we have in abundance to keep them interesting as they make repeat appearances at our meals.

Beet greens are something that we often just throw away, not realizing how good they can be! Harvesting food fresh from the garden makes me reluctant to throw anything away if there's the remotest possibility of eating it – which resulted in the invention of this salad one day.

While cleaning up after sending out beets in the CSA bins, I was unable to send the beet greens to the pigs and instead incorporated them into our community lunch.

Rachel Sacco

Salads & Dips

Apple Carrot Salad

¼ cup fresh lemon/lime juice
2 tbs orange juice
1 tbs honey
2 cups apple, peeled

2 cups carrots, shredded
1 tbs fresh mint, chopped
¼ cup craisins or raisins
Salt to taste

Prep Time
15 min

Serves
4-6

1. In a large bowl, mix juices and honey till honey is dissolved.
2. Grate apples directly into juice mixture to prevent apples from browning.
3. Toss remaining ingredients with apples and serve immediately.

adapted from Simply in Season

Beet Green Salad

Salad
1 bunch beet greens, coarsely chopped
1 bunch Swiss chard, coarsely chopped
Goat's cheese, crumbled
Apples, thinly sliced
Walnuts, chopped
Dried cranberries

Dressing
½ cup salad oil
¼ cup apple cider vinegar
¼ cup honey
1 tsp Dijon mustard

An excellent way to use an under-appreciated veggie!

Contributor: Rachel Sacco, Fall 2013 Sustainable Agriculture Intern at Brooksdale

Often you hear about leaving the pit of the avocado in the guacamole to prevent the avocado from turning black, and so that is how I always prepare my guacamole.

I have realised after making so many bowls of guacamole that it's not the pit that keeps the avocado from turning black, but the LIME juice! When I pack apple wedges in my children's lunch bags, I squeeze lime juice on them and that way, by the time they eat them at school, the apples are still good looking!

So, you can leave the avocado pits in for decoration if you want, it's up to you!

Sandra Gaglardi

Broccoli Salad

Prep Time
20 min

Serves
6

Salad
3 cups broccoli florets
1 cup craisins
½ cup sunflower seeds
½ cup walnuts
½ cup cheese (optional)

Dressing
2 tbs sugar
1 tbs apple cider vinegar
¾ cup plain yogurt or sour cream

1. Stir sugar and vinegar together till dissolved.
2. Add yogurt till well blended.
3. Pour over broccoli mixture and toss well.

Adapted from Simply in Season

Mexican Guacamole

Prep Time
15 min

Serves
8 - 10

5 ripe avocados
4-5 ripe roma tomatoes, diced
½ white onion, chopped
½ bunch cilantro, chopped

Juice of 1 ½ - 2 fresh limes
Salt to taste
2 - 3 Serrano peppers, finely chopped (optional)

1. Scoop out avocados and mash with fork or potato masher.
2. Add tomatoes, onions, cilantro, lime juice and salt, and mix well.
3. If you want some heat, add peppers as desired. For a really hot Mexican version, leave seeds and veins on peppers.
4. Serve with tortilla chips or on barbecue burgers!

TIP
When chopping peppers, wear latex gloves and avoid touching your eyes!

Contributor: Sandra Gaglardi, Accountant for ARC National Office

8

I have always aspired to grow tomatoes in great enough quantity that everyone would get as much as they need (and more). Alas, our cool, humid coastal climate is not conducive to growing masses of tomatoes. There are never enough when it comes to big tomato projects like salsa making.

Then I discovered tomatillos. They are in the same family as tomatoes, and are picked green and made into "Salsa Verde" - a traditional condiment in Mexican cuisine - more widely used than the chunky tomato based-salsas that most of us know and eat. They grow abundantly in our climate without the disease issues that plague tomatoes. Their tangy flavour is a bit of an acquired taste.

My family loves salsa verde, especially this version, with chipotle peppers (a chipotle is a dried, smoked Jalapeno), which can be found in Latin supermarkets or specialty stores.

Paul Neufeld

Roasted Tomatillo-Chipotle Salsa

2 lbs tomatillos
2-4 dried chipotle peppers
½ small onion, quartered
2-3 cloves garlic

1 tbs lime juice
½ tbs honey or sugar
¼ cup cilantro, finely chopped
Salt

Prep Time
30 min

1. Remove papery husks from tomatillos. Place them on a baking sheet and broil them on high for a few minutes till blistered. Puree in a food processor and strain the liquid.

2. In a heavy pan, fry chipotles for a few minutes till aroma is released (It can be pungent!).

3. Pour chipotles into a bowl and add some boiling water. Cover with a plate slightly smaller than the bowl rim to keep the chipotles submerged. Soak for 15 min.

4. Puree chipotles in a food processor, using as little of the water as you can. Keep leftover chipotle liquid (It's good for cooking bean dishes!).

5. Add rest of ingredients to pureed chipotle and blend together.

6. Add salt, lime juice and cilantro to taste.

7. Serve with corn chips, burritos, rice or beans!

Mass canning (15-20 pints) for Brooksdale kitchen!

25 lbs tomatillos
20 dried chipotle peppers
6 small onions, quartered
Vegetable oil
4-5 heads garlic

1 cup lime juice
¼ to ½ cup honey or sugar
4 tsp salt
3 cups corn
1-2 cups cilantro, chopped

1. Repeat steps 1, 2, 3 and 4 in the above recipe.

2. Toss onions in oil and roast in oven at 425°F / 218°C for 25 min till soft and golden brown.

3. Puree roasted onions with garlic.

4. Transfer all purees into a large pot and heat. Add remaining ingredients except cilantro and continue heating till mixture comes to a low boil. Add cilantro.

5. Can mixture in pressure canner: 10 lbs for 5 min (pint) or 10 min (quart).

Contributor: Paul Neufeld, Farm Manager at Brooksdale

One of my favourite tasks is to cook lunch in late summer or early fall at Brooksdale when the harvest is in surplus mode and there are veggies begging to get picked and processed. It gets my creative neurons firing and challenges me to work towards a delicious meal from mostly garden produce. Afterwards, the cycle of harvesting and preparing the meal is completed by a visit to the chickens or the compost pile with peelings and scraps.

Bettina Konrad

Tabouli Fusion Salad

1 cup brown basmati rice, rinsed
4 cups water
1 ½ tsp salt
1 cup parsley, finely chopped
½ cup onion greens/chives, finely chopped
1 ½ cups cucumber, diced
1 tbs mint, finely chopped
1 cup feta cheese, crumbled
½ tsp garlic, crushed
1 tsp grated lemon rind
2 tbs lemon juice
¼ cup olive oil
Salt and pepper to taste

Variation
Use quinoa or other cooked grains instead of rice!

Prep Time
1 h 15 min

Serves
6

1. Bring water and salt to boil.

2. Add basmati rice. Leave temperature on high until water is boiling again, then reduce heat and cover the rice with a lid. Cook for 50 min to an hour.

3. While the rice is cooking, prepare all the other ingredients.

4. When the rice is cooked, strain it, put it in cold water and strain it again till the excess water has drained away.

5. Put the rice and all the other ingredients in a bowl. Toss and add salt and pepper to taste.

The nice thing about this salad is that you can replace many ingredients based on what is in season.
Use other finely chopped herbs and greens in addition to what's mentioned such as basil, dill, spinach and peppers.

TIP
Use 1 tbs of finely chopped white onion to replace onion greens or chives.

The first time we were paired up for lunch duty, Cheryl and I decided on a Japanese theme – Japanese vegetable curry and a Japanese wafu salad. We planned around the vegetables coming out of our garden that week (potato, winter squash and carrots) and the plentiful supply of apples from our neighbours.

The night before, we found (to our horror) that the kitchen was out of soy sauce – the one ingredient that's quintessentially Japanese! We had to have soy sauce!

So we turned to Google for help and discovered that it's possible to make a soy sauce substitute! It also helped that our pantry was well stocked in bouillon cubes, balsamic vinegar, dark molasses, ground ginger and garlic powder. As we gathered these ingredients, I came to a hilarious realisation: Where else would you find Asians trying to make soy sauce substitute from scratch but at A Rocha?!

Although our concoction didn't taste exactly like soy sauce, we had great fun learning to make do with what we had and everyone enjoyed the food!

Pamela Soo

4 Salad Dressings

Honey Mustard Dressing

⅓ cup olive oil

⅓ cup honey

⅓ cup mustard

Creamy Dressing

1 garlic clove, chopped
⅓ cup mayonnaise
¼ cup plain yogurt
3 tbs cider vinegar

½ tsp sugar
½ tsp salt
Pepper
Fresh basil or chives

Wafu (Japanese style) Dressing

3 ½ tbs vegetable oil
3 ½ tbs soy sauce
3 tbs rice vinegar

½ tbs sesame seeds, roasted
¼ cup onion, grated (with juice)
Pepper

When chilled, it pairs well with lettuce or cabbage slaw!

Gingered Sesame Dressing

½ cup soy sauce
¼ cup brown sugar
2 tbs rice vinegar
2 tbs vegetable oil
1 tsp sesame oil

2 tbs orange juice
1 tbs ginger, minced
1 garlic clove, minced
3 tbs sesame seeds, roasted

Serve with salad or gluten-free soba noodles!

Adapted from http://justonecookbook.com/blog/recipes/wafu-dressing-japanese-salad-dressing/
and http://www.tasteofhome.com/recipes/soba-noodles-with-gingered-sesame-dressing

Contributor: Pamela Soo, Fall 2013 Environmental Education Intern at Brooksdale

14

The predominant theme overarching all the farming and eating at A Rocha's Centres has been one of abundance. Weekly Community Shared Agriculture (CSA) baskets (actually, big Rubbermaid blue tubs) overflow with up to twenty different selections of produce, from potatoes to spinach to rutabagas.

The bounty is so copious that most CSA members split their share with another household since they find it impossible to make it through all those veggies in one week.

Reflecting on this theme of abundance, our farmer Paul summed it up well in one of his regular CSA newsletters: "Such abundance is a gift, and makes possible other gifts: healthy bodies and minds nourished by good food; the raw materials for hospitality; the opportunity for generosity; the necessity of creativity in the kitchen (what to do with kohlrabi?); and the reminder that all of this comes from the hand of our generous Creator!"

Leah Kostamo, *Planted, A Story of Creation, Calling and Community*

Soups

Great is Thy faithfulness

Great is Thy faithfulness!
Great is Thy faithfulness!
Morning by morning new mercies I see;
All I have needed Thy hand hath provided;
Great is Thy faithfulness, Lord, unto me!

Basic Stock

Stock, or broth, refers to the liquid used as the base for soups. It is made by simmering vegetables and/or meat (even bones) in a pot for several hours. A homemade soup stock is a simple and economical way to add both flavour and nutrition to your food!

Great base ingredients

Celery (with leaves)   Mushrooms

Whole leeks   Carrots

Onions   Apples

Any greens

Herbs

Parsley   Bay leaves (earthy note)

Rosemary   Thyme (woody note)

1. Roughly chop vegetables. Peel skin as desired.
2. Lightly sauté aromatic vegetables like onions, celery and carrots to develop sweeter, more complex flavours.
3. In a large pot, add vegetables and generously cover with cold water (which helps to extract more flavour from stock ingredients).
4. Bring to a boil, then reduce heat to gently simmer for about 1 h. If the heat is too high, delicate flavours may boil off; if the heat is too low, not all flavours will be extracted.
5. Let cooked vegetables sit as stock cools down.

TIP
Mushrooms are high in natural glutamic acid which enhances food with a savoury, umami flavour!

A good culinary skill to learn especially since we make many soups at Brooksdale!

Adapted from http://thestonesoup.com/blog/2010/05/7-tips-for-full-flavoured-vegetable-stock/

Contributor: Paul Neufeld, Farm Manager at Brooksdale

18

The "important" thing... was not how good a rare and
expensive delicacy tasted, but how amazing ordinary food could
be if he paid close attention to each mouthful.

Mark Williams, John Teasdale, Zindel Segal and Jon Kabat-Zinn,
The Mindful Way Through Depression

Apple Pumpkin Soup

3 cups pumpkin, pureed

2 Granny Smith apples, sliced

2-4 cups chicken stock

2 garlic cloves, chopped

1 big onion, chopped

1 tbs fresh ginger, grated

1 ½ tbs vegetable oil

Salt and pepper to taste

Prep Time
10 min

Cooking Time
20 min

Serves
4

1. Heat oil in a saucepan over medium heat and sauté onions till translucent.
2. Add garlic and ginger. Stir for 1 min till fragrant.
3. Add pumpkin and stock and heat through.
4. Add apples and cook till tender.
5. Add salt and pepper to taste.

Curried Pumpkin Soup

1 tsp vegetable oil

¼ cup onions, chopped

1 tsp curry powder

3 cups chicken stock

3 cups pumpkin, peeled and cubed

1 can (14 ½ oz) diced tomatoes

⅓ cup frozen corn

Salt and pepper to taste

Prep Time
15 min

Cooking Time
40 min

Serves
4

Meat Variation
Add ¾ cup shredded chicken breast at the last step.

1. Heat the oil in a large saucepan over medium heat.
2. Add onions and cook till translucent.
3. Add curry and stir well till fragrant.
4. Add the stock, pumpkin and tomatoes. Bring to a boil.
5. Reduce heat and simmer for 10-15 min till pumpkin is tender.
6. Use an immersion blender or a food processor to puree the soup till smooth. You can skip this step for a more chunky soup.
7. Add corn and heat through. Add salt and pepper to taste.

It can be found in every culture and every country, in the hottest and coldest of climates. It can be made of glass, or stone or wood, or granite, or snowpack. It can be raised and balanced on four or more legs; it can only be slightly raised above the ground or floor level to convenience reclining or sitting on the floor or ground. It can be round, square, oval, oblong, rectangular, or flip out from the back of the airline seat in front of you.

It can be pounded in anger and used to brace a faltering resolve. Treachery and murder, war and devastation have been plotted on it, and peace treaties and commitments of love and fidelity have been signed upon it, as well. It can be a place of solitude and sadness, or a warm gathering-place of family and friends. It can be the centrepiece of a home or the cold and imposing centrepiece of a corporate boardroom. It can be the centre of nourishment and nurturing, or the background of unresolved conflict. Princes own one; paupers do as well.

It is the humble and often-overlooked TABLE.

Sandra Manning

Beet Borscht Soup

5 cups broth, any flavour

2 cups beets, thinly sliced

½ cups potatoes, thinly sliced

½ cups onion, chopped

stalk celery, chopped

carrot, sliced

3-4 cups cabbage, shredded

I tsp dill (and more for garnish)

2 tbs vinegar or cider/red wine

2 tbs honey or brown sugar

I cup tomato puree

Salt and pepper

Prep Time
30 min

Cooking Time
I h IO min

Serves
4

1. In a medium pot, cook beets and potatoes in broth over medium heat for 20-30 min till tender.

2. In a pan, sauté onions in butter over medium heat till translucent.

3. Add celery, carrots, cabbage and a few cups of broth to prevent vegetables from sticking. Cook till vegetables are tender.

4. Add remaining ingredients. Cover and simmer for at least 15 min.

5. Taste and adjust seasonings as desired.

Borscht is one of those dishes that can be made with what you have! The exact proportions are not too fussy - no need to measure exactly!

The industrial eater is, in fact, one who does not know that eating is an agricultural act, who no longer knows or imagines the connection between eating and the land, and who is therefore necessarily passive and uncritical - in short, a victim.

Wendell Berry, "The Pleasures of Eating"

Creamy Lentil Soup

6 cups vegetable/chicken broth
2 cups French green lentils, rinsed
2 bay leaves
1 whole clove

Prep Time
30 min

Cooking Time
45 min

Serves
6-8

1. Combine all ingredients in a large pot and bring to a boil.
2. Reduce heat, cover and simmer for 25-30 min till lentils are tender. Set aside.

2 tbs butter
1 medium onion, chopped
3 celery ribs, chopped
2 medium carrots, chopped
3 garlic cloves, minced
1 ½ cups whipping cream
1 tbs lemon juice
3 cups bok choy, coarsely chopped
⅓ cup cilantro, chopped

Seasoning:
1 tsp salt
1 tsp sugar
⅛ tsp pepper
½ - 1 tsp curry powder

TIP
Substitute bok choy with kale or spinach - all are very tasty!

3. Sauté first four ingredients in a pan till crispy tender.
4. Add seasoning and sauté for 3 min till tender.
5. Add garlic and sauté garlic for 1 min.
6. Add vegetable mixture to the lentil soup and discard bay leaves.
7. Stir in whipping cream and lemon juice and simmer over low heat.
8. Add bok choy and cilantro. Simmer till heated through and bok choy is wilted.

"Let us be satisfied" - that's it in a nutshell, isn't it? It's all about satisfaction, or the lack of it. The perpetual desire for satisfaction is what drives our consumerism and ultimately puts our planet at risk and at the same time impoverishes so many in this country and around the world. What the psalmist and my friends see is that we will never get out from underneath our powerful wrongs until we can be satisfied, not with getting more (as we have all been trained to want), but rather with the steady flow of goodness that comes from God.

Ellen F. Davis, *God the Farmer* referring to Psalm 65, especially Psalm 65:4.

Rutabaga and Squash Curry Soup

4 tsp olive oil

1 onion, chopped

3 cloves garlic, minced

1 carrot, diced

1 rib celery, diced or ½ cup celeriac

1 tbs fresh ginger, grated

¼ tsp pepper

1 ½ tsp Thai red curry paste*

4 cups rutabaga, peeled and cubed

4 cups winter squash, peeled and cubed

400 ml coconut milk

½ cup pot barley

4-5 cups water

2 stock cubes

1 ½ cups mushrooms, sliced

3 cups greens (e.g. Tah Tsai, spinach, Swiss chard, kale)

1 tbs lime juice

Prep Time
25 min

Cooking Time
35 min

Serves
6

1. In a large saucepan, sauté onion, garlic, carrots and celery in oil till tender.

2. Add ginger, pepper and curry paste. Sauté for another 2 min.

3. Add rutabaga, winter squash, coconut milk and barley.

4. Add water till all ingredients are submerged and add stock cubes (or cover with stock). Bring to a boil, then reduce heat and simmer for 40 min.

5. In another saucepan, sauté mushrooms and set aside.

6. Prior to serving, add mushrooms, lime juice and greens. Let stand for 2 min till the greens wilt.

*Add more curry paste for extra heat!

Adapted from Canadian Living Magazine "Curry Vegetable Barley Soup"

Contributor: Katie Wood, Schoolyard Farm Coordinator at Brooksdale

"The shared meal elevates eating from a mechanical process of fueling the body to a ritual of family and community, from mere animal biology to an act of culture."

Michael Pollan, *In Defense of Food*

Mains

The first time I made this dish, we were new to living and working for A Rocha and I was cooking lunch for 35+ people, which was intimidating to me. Someone suggested that I cook beans and rice and that was exactly what I did....and nothing else.

We had a newborn baby at the time and so my creativity for coming up with ideas was minimal. There was no salsa or sour cream or veggies or even cheese(!!), but it was still a hit and a good reminder of how the majority of the world eats on a daily basis.

Five years and many new toppings later, I am still having a lot of fun playing with this dish and it never fails to be well received at centre meals!

Roxy Humphrey

Black Beans & Rice

I cup dried black beans, soaked overnight
3-4 cups water
I bouillon cube, any flavour
1-2 bay leaves
2 cups rice
2 tbs vegetable oil
I onion, diced

1 - 2 peppers
Half a cabbage, chopped/diced
Fresh lettuce
Fresh cilantro, chopped
Salsa/diced tomatoes
Sour cream/yogurt
Cheddar cheese, grated

Prep Time
30 min

Cooking Time
2h 15 min

Serves
4

1. Drain water from soaked black beans.
2. Simmer the black beans in 3-4 cups water along with the bouillon cube and bay leaves for 2h or until most of the water has evaporated and the beans are soft. If the beans are not soft enough, then add more water and keep cooking.
3. Cook the rice separately in a covered pot on the stove or in a rice cooker (follow the cooking instructions for the type of rice you use).
4. Sauté onions in oil till translucent.
5. Add peppers and cabbage and cook for 5 min.
6. Serve separately the beans, rice, sautéed veggies and all the other ingredients listed.

Variation
You can make baked potatoes instead of rice.

This is a great meal for people who have various dietary restrictions, as they can serve themselves and include or exclude various items based on their own diets.

In The Lord I'll Be Ever Thankful

In the Lord I'll be ever thankful,
In the Lord I will rejoice!
Look to God, do not be afraid.
Lift up your voices, the Lord is near,
Lift up your voices, the Lord is near.

Taizé

Fried Rice

2 tbs vegetable oil
2 eggs
4 cloves garlic, minced
shallot, minced
carrot, grated/diced
½ small green or purple
cabbage, sliced

¼ tsp salt
2 cups overnight cooked rice
1 bell pepper, diced
2 tbs soy sauce
¼ tsp pepper
Cilantro, chopped

Prep Time
20 min

Cooking Time
5 min

Serves
4

1. Heat ½ tbs oil in pan and scramble eggs. Set aside.
2. Add remaining oil in pan. Stir-fry garlic and shallot till golden.
3. Add carrot and cabbage. Stir-fry for 1 min.
4. Add salt and stir well.
5. Add rice and stir well till rice is evenly mixed with vegetables.
6. Add eggs and bell pepper.
7. Add 2tbs of soy sauce and pepper. Stir well.
8. Serve with cilantro on top.

TIP
Leftover /
overnight rice is
best for cooking
fried rice as the
rice grains will not
turn mushy
during cooking.

Variations
Fried Rice is versatile!
1. Use any seasonal
vegetables like bok choy, corn,
kale, peas, Swiss chard, etc.
Have fun experimenting!
Just remember to cook the
hardier vegetables first.
2. Use leftover turkey, chicken,
salmon, beef or pork for
extra protein.

Contributor: Shai Kroeker, 2011 Environmental Education Intern at Brooksdale

Pizza is my favourite meal to make. My friends and family know that when I invite them for dinner, the chances are good that I will be serving them some crazy off-beat pizza. This recipe is my favourite, which I created one summer night when preparing for a BBQ when I only had beets, Swiss chard and onion in my veggie drawer in my fridge.
It was a major hit!

When coming as an intern to A Rocha in Sept 2013, part of our internship included visiting a farm on Galiano Island for four days and staying with the very hospitable Mary-Ruth and Loren Wilkinson. Here we learned about hospitality and food: the theme of our stay was "Taste and See" and it was a beautiful time of connecting my faith, and my understanding of the character of God, to the sacredness of shared meals and hospitality.

I made this pizza in the Wilkinson's outside cob oven on a cold, blustering and rainy September day; warm, shared pizza hit the spot!

Sarah Duncan

Gourmet Caramelized Onion, Beet and Swiss Chard Spelt Pizza

Dough

1 cup hot water
7 g quick dry yeast
1 tbs olive oil
1 tbs honey
Pinch of salt
1 cup all-purpose/whole wheat flour
1 ½ cups spelt flour

Toppings

3 red beets, peeled and sliced
1 big onion, chopped
3 tbs balsamic vinegar
1 tbs brown sugar
A handful Swiss chard
½ - 1 cup cheddar cheese, grated
Salt and pepper to taste
3 cloves garlic, pressed
1 tbs butter

Prep Time
30 min

Cooking Time
15 min

Serves
4

1. Preheat the oven at 450°F / 230°C.

2. In large bowl, stir together hot water and yeast. Add oil, honey and salt. Slowly add the flours and knead lightly with hands. Add more flour if dough turns sticky.

3. Mix into a ball and let the dough sit in a covered bowl and in a warm place for 10-20 min.

4. Sauté onions in olive oil on medium heat till tender.

5. Add vinegar and sugar. Reduce heat to low, stirring occasionally, and simmer for about 15 min.

6. In another pan, sauté beets in olive oil till softened. Add salt and pepper as desired. Add Swiss chard and cook till reduced.

7. In a small bowl, mix garlic and butter to make garlic butter.

[Continued]

8. Sprinkle flour on a greased pizza pan. Roll/stretch dough onto the pan.
9. Spread garlic butter evenly on dough.
10. Sprinkle caramelized onions, followed by cheddar cheese. Then, layer on cooked beets and Swiss chard. Finally, place the beets on top of the pizza like pepperoni.
11. Bake for 12-14 min. The crust should be just barely browned for best tasting pizza dough!
12. Leave to cool for 5 min, then slice and serve.

TIP
No worries about being fancy. Use your fingers to make the dough spread evenly across the pan if it's sticky.

It's great if served with a fresh green salad and a Shiraz red wine.

Contributor: Sarah Duncan, 2013 Fall Sustainable Agriculture Intern at Brooksdale

My first attempt ever at making pizza dough from scratch was during a Farm To Family program, which connects low-income families to food, community and Creation.

I asked, "Who likes pizza?" and everyone at the table — both kids and parents — raised their hands in glee! We spent the next half an hour preparing the dough, slicing Swiss chard from the Kids' Garden, grating mozarella cheese to create pizza masterpieces.

Five minutes in the cob oven and there we go - three sizzling pizzas served complete with cheesy fingers and satisfied faces. It was truly a delight to watch them savour the fresh food they had just made!

Pamela Soo

As a family and at A Rocha we try to eat real food from a bit lower on the food chain. It's our meager stand of solidarity with our brothers and sisters in the two-thirds world for whom a locally grown, mostly vegetarian diet is the norm. Most long-term guests take our food agenda in stride, or at least they try to.

In the beginning lentils are novel, and they feel noble eating like the rest of the two-thirds world. But after a week or two this wears off and there is a clamouring for meat - big chunks of it. In this case, I'm reminded of one of our first A Rocha interns, Martin Lings. I was in charge of the food during the early days of our Environmental Centre and while I'm not a terrible cook, I was run a bit off my feet and my cooking suffered as a result.

I recall one particular day when I had morphed leftover lentils into their third incarnation. This simple little act of efficiency caused Martin, normally the height of English civility, to positively lose it. The scene went something like this:

ME, sauntering to the table with a child on my hip and casserole dish in hand (the very picture of female domesticity):
"Dinner's served!"

MARTIN, staring hungrily from the table:
"Smells good, what's for tea (read: supper)?"

ME, coyly: "Oh, just a little lentil thing I refashioned."

MARTIN, face falling, eyeing the casserole dish suspiciously: "Huh?"

ME, smiling a bit too brightly. No comment as I lift the casserole lid.

MARTIN, wailing: "Nooooooo, not Lentil Goo again!"

Indeed, it was Lentil Goo again! But in the years since I have perfected Lentil Goo into Lentil Dahl, which, if I do say so myself, is rather tasty.

Leah Kostamo

Leah's Dahl

2 onions, chopped
Olive oil
4 tbs curry powder
4 tbs ground cumin
3 tbs ground coriander
2 tbs garam marsala

1 tsp ground cardamom
2 heaping tbs brown sugar
2 tbs salt
5 cups red lentils
10 cups water

Prep Time
10 min

Cooking Time
1h 15 min

Serves
8

1. In a saucepan, sauté onions in plenty of olive oil.

2. Add spices, sugar and salt.

3. Add red lentils and water and bring to a boil. Turn heat down to simmer for 1 h, stirring every once in a while. Add more water if needed as dahl cooks.

4. Taste and add more spices as desired.

5. Serve on rice, with plain yogurt and chutney.

For a couple of years it became a weekly standard at the A Rocha table and was almost always appreciated even by the more carnivorous in the crowd. I offer you now, a sketch of that dish!

Sometimes, I end up more than doubling the spices and salt, because I've just "eyeballed" it to start with.

Johnny Appleseed Grace, a favourite among A Rocha kids

The Lord is good to me,
and so I thank the Lord,
for giving me the things I need,
the sun and the rain and the apple seed,
the Lord is good to me.
Johnny Appleseed.
Amen!

Palak Paneer

Prep Time
30 min

Cooking Time
30 min

Serves
4

2 tbs ghee or vegetable oil
1 onion, chopped
1 lb paneer, cubed
4 cloves garlic, chopped
2 tbs fresh ginger root, grated
2 dried red chilli peppers (optional)
4 tsp garam masala powder
4 tsp ground cumin

2 tsp ground coriander
2 tsp ground turmeric
3 lb spinach, chopped
1 large tomato, chopped
3/4 cup cream or sour cream
8 sprigs fresh cilantro leaves
Salt and pepper to taste
3 bay leaves
1 cup cashew nuts (optional)

1. Heat 1 tbs ghee or oil in pan. Add cubed paneer and sauté until brown. Set aside the paneer.

2. Heat 1 tbs ghee or oil in pan. Sauté onion until light golden brown.

3. When onions are browned, add garlic, ginger and red chillies. Sauté 2 min.

4. Add garam masala, cumin, coriander, turmeric and sauté briefly.

5. Add spinach, cover with lid and cook down.

6. When spinach is cooked down, add tomatoes, cream and half of cilantro. Cook for a few minutes.

7. Blend spinach mixture (in blender or hand wand) and return to pan. Add salt and pepper to taste.

8. Add bay leaves and paneer to spinach. Cook for about 10 min in medium heat.

9. Garnish with remaining cilantro and cashews nuts.

10. Serve with rice and/or naan.

TIP
Toast dry ground cumin & coriander first for a more aromatic flavour.

Paneer is a type of fresh cheese and widely used in Indian cuisine. You can make it at home using milk, lemon juice & salt.

Pumpkin Lasagne

1 pumpkin, quartered/eighthed
1 medium onion, chopped
2 cloves garlic, pressed
1 ½ tbs vegetable oil
1 can (28 oz) diced tomatoes
1 tbs brown sugar
½ tsp pumpkin pie spice mix ✱
Salt and pepper

2 ½ cups ricotta cheese
1 cup mozzarella cheese, shredded
½ cup Romano cheese, shredded
1 egg
250 ml whipping cream
1-2 packs No-boil lasagna noodles
Extra cup of cheddar/Romano cheese, shredded

1. Preheat the oven at 400°F / 200°C.
2. Place pumpkin (cut side down) on a baking dish. Add some water and cover with aluminium foil. Bake for 30-45 min, depending on pumpkin size, till tender.
3. Leave to cool. Remove the pumpkin skin and cut into thin slices.
4. To prepare the tomato sauce, sauté onion and garlic in oil till translucent. Add diced tomatoes, brown sugar and spices. Stir well. Add salt and pepper to taste.
5. To prepare the cheese, mix the cheeses, egg and whipping cream in another bowl.
6. In a greased 9" x 13" baking dish, add in this order: ¼ tomato sauce. a layer of lasagne noodles, ¼ tomato sauce, a layer of pumpkin slices, ½ cheese mixture, a layer of lasagne noodles, ¼ tomato sauce, a layer of pumpkin slices, remaining cheese mixture and a layer of lasagne noodles. Spread remaining tomato sauce on top.

TIP
You could use pumpkin puree if you prefer a softer texture!

[Continued]

7. Sprinkle the extra cup of cheddar/Romano cheese on top.
8. Cover with foil and bake for 30 min. Remove foil and bake for another 10-15 min till cheese is bubbling and slightly brown.
9. Leave to cool for 15 min before serving.

✱ Pumpkin Pie Spice Mix from scratch:
½ tsp ground cinnamon
¼ tsp ground ginger
⅛ tsp ground all spice or cloves
⅛ tsp ground nutmeg

Ute developed the Pumpkin Lasagne recipe for a bigger crowd, so the measurements featured here are a rough estimate. Have fun and play around to your liking!

At the 2013 Harvest Celebration, she made a Cinderella Pumpkin Lasagne for food tasting. It was a huge hit, and the recipe was featured by demand in the CSA newsletter the following week.

Quiche is a simple dish that allows you to fully express your creativity! Almost any vegetable can join or replace meat, a great opportunity to make the most of the sometimes overwhelming diversity provided by A Rocha's garden.

As for me, my favourite remains the original Quiche Lorraine, with a nice graded Swiss cheese on top. In that case, you don't want to forget a large nice green salad to go on the side... Bon appétit!

David Nussbaumer

Quiche Lorraine

2 ½ cups flour

⅔ cup butter, at room temperature

½ tsp salt

8 ml warm water

200 g ham, sliced or bacon, diced

3 eggs

200 ml milk

20 ml half & half cream

Salt, pepper and ground nutmeg to taste

Extra Toppings
Mushrooms, leeks, broccoli, spinach, cheese, etc.

Grated cheese is highly recommended! Goat cheese can give a very unique taste!

Prep Time
1 h

Cooking Time
1 h

Serves
3-4

Pastry

1. In a bowl, mix flour and salt.
2. Add butter and mix gently but quickly with your fingertips for about 2-3 min.
3. Quickly add water and mix till a ball of dough is formed (very little water is needed).
4. Roll out pastry on a light floured surface.

TIP
Take the butter out of the fridge 3 h before starting to cook, or put in the microwave on lowest setting for 10 sec at a time till softened, not liquid.

Quiche

5. Preheat the oven at 350°F / 180°C.
6. Line pastry in a greased springform or round tart tin and press. Lightly prick the base with a fork all over.
7. Spread ham (or fried bacon) on pastry. Add extra toppings of your choice.
8. In a bowl, mix eggs, milk and cream. Add salt, pepper and nutmeg as desired.
9. Pour mixture over the toppings.
10. Bake for 45-50 min.

Adapted from www.marmiton.org

Contributor: David Nussbaumer, Summer 2013 Conservation Intern at Brooksdale

When I made these burgers for the first time on a Volunteer Day,
a little boy came to me after he finished his first burger and asked
for a second one. He said he never would have thought that
vegetable burgers could taste so good.

That is always the highlight of my cooking day, when people come
to me and ask for the recipes (which is tricky, since I rarely work
with recipes). I also love it when young children come and ask for
second helpings; they're normally full with one portion, so the
second one is just because they like it so much.

Ute Lindenlauf

Root Cellar Burger

½ cup sesame seeds
½ cup sunflower seeds
½ cup pumpkin seeds
3 cups beets, grated
1 ½ cups carrots, grated
½ cup parsnip, grated
½ cup onion, chopped
2 eggs

1 cup brown rice, cooked
½ cup canola oil
½ cup parsley, chopped
3 tbs flour
2 tbs soy sauce
2 cloves garlic, minced
A dash of cayenne
Salt and pepper to taste

Prep Time
45 min

Cooking Time
25 min

Serves
12

1. Toast all seeds in a skillet on the stove for 3-5min.

2. Preheat oven to 350°F / 180°C.

3. Combine all ingredients in a bowl and mix thoroughly. (You may want to add a bit more flour if it is too runny. It can be messy as the dough is softer than meat burgers.)

4. Shape into patties and bake for about 25 min till edges are browned.

5. Best served with toasted buns and favourite condiments!

TIP
For extra large and thick patties, flip them over to bake evenly.

Variation
Slice 1/3 of pumpkin,
instead of cubing, and
parboil. Fry with additional
oil, cumin and salt, till
brown and crisp. Add on
top of curry when
serving.

This recipe is one that I thought up during my undergraduate degree in England. It's as easy to make for a large number of people that you've invited to a Christian Union event as it is for a small meal with special friends or your family.

I find it ideal to use whatever vegetables you happen to have or are in season. I've cooked it many times now and it's been different every time! I've called the recipe "'Pumpkin Curry", but you can use winter squash, sweet potato or even a mixture.

Stephanie Bryant

Steph's Pumpkin & Chickpea Curry

4-5 cups pumpkin, peeled and cubed
1 cup chickpeas, soaked overnight
2 cups of seasonal vegetables, chopped
½ cup onions, chopped
400 ml coconut milk
¼ vegetable stock cube, crumbled

2-3 tbs vegetable oil
1 tbs ground cumin
½ tbs cumin seeds
2 tsp ground coriander
1 tsp garam masala
1 tsp turmeric
1 tsp salt

Prep Time
40 min

Cooking Time
1 h 30 min

Serves
4

1. Drain soaked chickpeas. Cook chickpeas in a pot by covering with hot water and boil till soft for 1 h. Drain water and set aside.
2. Parboil pumpkin in a large pot till softened. Drain water.
3. Heat oil in a large pot on medium-low heat. Add ground cumin, cumin seeds, garam masala, ground coriander and turmeric.
4. Add onions and a pinch of salt. Sauté on medium heat.
5. Add coconut milk, chickpeas and vegetables (those with longer cooking times first). Simmer till vegetables are soft.
6. Add pumpkin, crumbled stock cube and salt to taste. Simmer till curry starts to thicken as desired.
7. Serve with rice.

TIP
Taste and add more spices if you desire a stronger or spicier taste.

Coconut milk can vary greatly in consistency. Usually the cream separates from the liquid in the can. I tend to add the cream to the curry first, then the liquid as required. If you need more liquid, make up a small amount of vegetable stock.

My favourite A Rocha food memory was the time when Shai used all the "rare" Asian delicacies to make lunch. What a shock it was to head over to the main house from the office and find out that a certain A Rocha pig was being served as the main course for lunch. She gave us a real orientation to pig heart, liver and even the ear!

Luke Wilson

Stuffed Winter Squash

Prep Time
30 min

Cooking Time
1 h

Serves
4

3 medium winter squash, halved lengthwise and seeds removed
3 tbs unsalted butter, melted
1 tbs packed dark brown sugar
½ medium onion, chopped
2 medium shallots, chopped
4 celery stalks, chopped
Salt and pepper to taste
1 tbs fresh thyme leaves, minced

2 cups rice, cooked
⅔ cup pecans, toasted and chopped
¼ cup dried cranberries, chopped

Winter squash is rich in antioxidants and healthy omega-3 fats!

1. Preheat the oven at 450°F / 230°C.
2. Place squash, cut side up, on a baking sheet. Brush with 1 tsp butter, sprinkle brown sugar and season with salt and pepper.
3. Bake for 25-30 min till just fork tender.
4. In a large frying pan, add 1 tbs melted butter on medium heat. When it foams, add onions, shallots and celery. Season with salt and pepper, and stir continuously for about 5 min till vegetables are softened.
5. Stir in thyme and cook for about 1 min till fragrant.
6. Remove pan from heat and stir in rice, pecans and cranberries.
7. Divide rice filling among roasted squash halves (about ½ cup) and drizzle remaining butter on top. Continue baking for 20-25 min till squash is completely fork tender and edges have started to brown.

Variation
Add grated cheese on top after baking rice filling for 10-15 min.

Adapted from http://www.chow.com/recipes/13566-roasted-acorn-squash-with-wild-rice-stuffing
Contributor: Queenie Hewitt, Community Garden Mobilizer for A Rocha Canada

Ubi Caritas

Ubi caritas et amor
Ubi caritas, Deus ibi est.

Where charity and love are,
God is there.

Torta Rustica

1 pack 10" tortillas
1 cup pesto
3 cups mozzarella cheese, grated
1 cup goat cheese
1 eggplant
2 zucchinis
4 bell peppers
2 yams
2 potatoes
2 red onions
¼ cup olive oil
1 tbs rosemary

Tomato sauce
10 tomatoes, quartered
1 red onion, diced
3 cloves garlic
¼ cup olive oil
1 tbs brown sugar
1 tsp chipotle sauce
¼ cup cilantro, chopped

Aioli
1 cup mayonnaise
Juice of 1 lemon
½ cup fresh basil, chopped
2 garlic cloves, pressed

Prep Time
30 min

Cooking Time
1 h 30 min

Serves
12

1. Preheat oven at 350°F / 180°C.

2. Slice all vegetables, then mix with olive oil and rosemary till finely coated.

3. Grill in oven for about 20 min till soft.

4. In a deep baking tray, assemble torta layers. Between each tortilla, spread one type of roasted vegetable, some of each cheese and a little pesto. For the top layer, coat with olive oil and mozzarella.

5. Bake, with cover, for 50-60 min at 350°F / 180°C.

6. To make sauce: Toss tomatoes, onion, garlic, oil and sugar. Roast in oven for 30 min at 350°F / 180°C till caramelized. Puree in food processor, then add chipotle and cilantro.

7. To make aioli, mix all ingredients.

8. To serve: Spoon some warm sauce on a plate, set a slice of torta on top and drizzle with aioli.

Adapted from White Water Cooks by Shelley Adams

Contributor: Philip Baskin, Fall 2013 Environmental Education Intern & Spring 2014 Conservation Intern at Cooksdale

I was very excited to participate in the A Rocha summer boat trip to Galiano Island! Audrey, Emma, Ed and I were on the team for preparing the first lunch! With very little time to prepare on arrival, we needed to plan a simple but hearty meal for everyone who would be VERY hungry as our first meal was at 6.30am in the morning. We thought everybody loves peanut butter and we had an amazing variety of fresh vegetables from the garden.

Voila! Twisted Gado Gado! We married my knowledge of the traditional Indonesian dish Gado Gado with the freshest vegetables from the garden at Brooksdale and had made the Almost Perfect Peanut Sauce the night before. Vegetables were also pre-cut.

In the shortest possible time, we had a sumptuous and nutritious Asian lunch that was the perfect start to a highly memorable trip!

Shai Kroeker

Twisted Gado Gado

1 pack rice stick noodles OR
5 bundles glass noodles/bean thread vermicelli
1 cucumber, sliced
3 tomatoes, wedged
5 carrots, in short strips   ½ cabbage, in short strips
1 bag of bean sprouts   A handful of snap peas
1 cauliflower, in florets   A handful of string beans, in short
1 broccoli crown, in florets   strips

Prep Time
30 min

Cooking Time
30 min

Serves
10

1. Cut all vegetables. Blanch each vegetable (except cucumber & tomatoes) in boiling water or steam for 1-2 min till crisp tender. If you prefer to have the vegetables raw, no blanching is required.

2. Cook noodles in boiling water for 6-8 min till soft. Glass noodles will turn transparent when cooked.

3. Serve ingredients individually or put blanched vegetables together in one bowl.

4. After assembling ingredients on a plate, pour Almost Perfect Peanut Sauce (next page) over it.

TIP
Steam blanching takes about 1 ½ times longer than water blanching.

"I named it Twisted Gado Gado because in place of rice, I have used noodles. The great thing about this dish is that you can use any seasonal vegetables or your favourite vegetables. If you love eggs and toufu like I do, put them in :) The quantity for each vegetable can be adjusted easily. Just note that when you put everything together, it is quite a substantial meal. "

Gado-Gado literally means mix-mix in Bahasa Indonesia. It is an Indonesian dish of boiled vegetables served with a peanut sauce dressing and lontong or ketupat, also known as glutinous rice cake.

Almost Perfect Peanut Sauce

2 cups peanut butter (natural, no sugar added kind)
⅓ cup soy sauce
½ cup brown sugar

½ cup fresh lemon/lime juice
2 cups water
8 cloves garlic

1. Blend all ingredients in food processor.
2. In a saucepan, heat mixture over medium heat till sauce begins to bubble and thicken. Stir regularly to prevent burning.
3. Serve hot or cold.

Optional
2 cups coconut milk
Ginger
Lemon grass, thinly sliced
Red chilli flakes to taste

Contributor: Shai Kroeker, 2011 Environmental Education Intern at Brooksdale

Vegetarian Pad Thai

pack rice stick noodles
cups hot water
-3 tbs fish sauce
cup ketchup
tbs molasses
-3 tbs sugar
cup soy sauce
tbs sweet chilli sauce
tsp hot sauce
cup vegetable oil

4 cloves garlic, pressed
3 eggs, lightly beaten
2 cups bean sprouts
1 bunch chives, chopped
2 carrots, peeled and grated
¾ cup cilantro, chopped
½ cup peanuts, roasted and chopped
1 lime, cut into wedges for garnish

Prep Time
30 min

Cooking Time
45 min

Serves
6

1. In a large bowl, add noodles and cover with hot (not boiling) water. Let sit for 30 min.
2. In a small bowl, combine fish sauce, ketchup, molasses, sugar, soy sauce, chilli sauce and hot sauce. Set sauce aside.
3. Drain noodles and set aside.
4. In a large pan, add some oil and stir-fry garlic over medium heat till golden. Add beaten eggs and stir constantly till dry. Set aside.
5. Heat remaining oil in pan. Add and stir fry noodles over medium heat for 4-5 min till shiny.
6. Add eggs, bean sprouts, chives, carrots, ½ cup cilantro and sauce. Stir to heat through.
7. Serve with remaining cilantro, chopped peanuts and lime wedges.

Adapted from Simply Love: A Family Cookbook by Ginny Love

Contributor: Shauna Anderson, Outreach Projects Coordinator & Brooksdale Centre Co-director

56

The psalm reminds us that we cannot honour God at the macro level, as Creator, if we are not also honouring God at the micro level, in the ways that we live and work and eat from the good earth that God has made. The myriad small actions that make up daily life are our most essential acts of worship - which literally means 'acknowledging God as worthy.'

We all, individually and corporately, need to ask how we may praise God more fully and sincerely as we drive, or eat, or invest our retirement funds, or shop for food and clothing, or heat and cool the house and the sanctuary.

Ellen F. Davis, *God the Farmer*

Veggie Shepherd's Pie

1 tbs olive oil

1 large onion, chopped

2 garlic cloves, minced

1 kg (2.2 lbs) potatoes, peeled and chopped

1 can (28 oz) diced or crushed tomatoes

2 large carrots, peeled and chopped

2 tbs thyme

1 vegetable stock cube, crumbled

1 cup dried lentils, cooked

2 tbs butter

A splash of milk

A handful of chives, chopped

⅔ cup cheese, grated (e.g. cheddar)

Salt & pepper to taste

Prep Time
30 min

Cooking Time
1 h 10 min

Serves
4

1. In a large sauce pan, heat olive oil, onion and garlic together till golden.

2. Boil potatoes for 10-15 min till soft.

3. Drain potatoes and return to pot. Add butter and milk and mash together. Add more butter, milk, salt and pepper to taste.

4. Add tomatoes, carrots, thyme and stock cube to onion mixture. Simmer for 10 min. If ingredients stick to pan, add some water, but don't submerge vegetables.

5. Add lentils and simmer for another 10 min.

6. Preheat the oven at 400°F / 190°C.

7. If lentil and vegetable filling is too watery, drain some liquid out. Place filling into a deep baking dish and spread mashed potatoes evenly on top. Sprinkle chives and cheese.

8. Bake covered for 25 min, and then uncovered for a further 15 min till the cheese is melted and golden.

TIP
Add cumin and fresh/dried chilli for extra flavour at step 5.

Did you know Shepherd's Pie is traditionally cooked with ground lamb, whereas cottage pie is with ground beef? So technically, this dish is neither!

Contributor: Emily Upcott, 2013 Conservation Intern at Brooksdale

Through being a Sustainable Agriculture Intern at A Rocha, I learned a lot about our relationship to what we eat. I learned that growing food is not easy and requires dedication and a love of seeing things grow and flourish.

There were tough days, but also many joyful days when I experienced, as Alfred Austin puts it, the full "glory of gardening: hands in the dirt, head in the sun, and heart with nature. To nurture a garden is to feed not just the body, but the soul."

When it came to Fridays, my day to cook, I knew it was all worth it when I could go to the garden, or the root cellar, and harvest some vegetables that I helped grow and make them into (hopefully!) delicious food - food that I knew had been grown well - and then sit down at the table with people who I had grown to care about to share in the abundance of creation.

Thomas Merton says, "From the moment you put a piece of bread in your mouth you are part of the world... You are in relationship with all who brought it to the table. We are least separate and most in common when we eat and drink."

Zoe Matties

Zoe's Beautiful Beet Burgers

2 cups beets, grated

2 cups carrots, grated

2 cups turnips, grated

½ cup onion, chopped

½ cup sunflower seeds

2 eggs, lightly beaten

1 cup rice or oatmeal, cooked

1 cup cheddar cheese, grated

½ cup olive oil

3 tsp flour

2 tbs soy sauce

2 cloves garlic, chopped

Prep Time
30 min

Cooking Time
20 min

Serves
14 patties

1. Preheat the oven at 350°F / 180°C.
2. Combine all ingredients and mix thoroughly.
3. Use your hands to form the mixture into patties and transfer to greased baking tray.
4. Bake for about 20 min till brown around edges.
5. Serve as they are or with bun and burger sides.

Variation
Use gluten-free flour or rice flour.

Variation
For a twist, add any extra grated root vegetables or squash you have lying around. If using zucchini, remember to squeeze out all the liquid!

Contributor: Zoe Matties, Fall 2012 Sustainable Agriculture & Summer 2013 Education Intern at Brooksdale

3 Gluten-free Staples

White Rice
On the stove

¼ - ⅓ cup dried white rice per person

1. Measure out desired amount of rice.
2. Optional: For jasmine rice, rinse once with cold water and drain well to reduce extra starch.
3. In a pot, add rice and double the amount of water. (1 cup of white rice : 2 cups of water). Cover with lid.
4. Bring to a complete boil (lid will start rattling and bubbling over).
5. Turn off heat and leave covered on stove for about 15 min (don't be tempted to remove lid before that).

Note: Brown rice requires more water (ratio 1 : 2 ½) and a longer time to cook.

Tip
If you burn your pot, don't fret! Add some water and baking soda, then bring to boil and simmer on medium heat. Or add some vinegar and leave overnight to do its magic!

Quinoa

1 cup dried quinoa = 1 ¼ cups cooked quinoa

1. Measure out desired amount of quinoa.
2. Rinse with water and drain well.
3. In a pot, add quinoa and double the amount of water. (1 cup of quinoa : 2 cups of water).
4. Bring to a boil, then turn heat on low, cover and cook for 15 min till water is absorbed.
5. Let cool for 5 min, fluff with fork and serve.

Note: Add stock cube(s) for a savoury version.

Soba/Buckwheat Noodles
Approx. 80 grams per person

1. Measure out desired amount of soba.
2. Bring a large pot of water to boil, then add noodles. Stir gently to ensure they are immersed.
3. Simmer according to time stated in package instructions.
4. Once cooked, drain noodles into colander and return to pot filled with cold water. Rinse noodles well.
5. Optional: Serve warm/cold with ginger sesame dressing.

Desserts

Eating with the fullest pleasure - pleasure, that is, that does not depend on ignorance - is perhaps the profoundest enactment of our connection with the world. In this pleasure we experience and celebrate our dependence and our gratitude, for we are living from mystery, from creatures we did not make and powers we cannot comprehend.

Wendell Berry, "The Pleasures of Eating"

Apple Cake

2 cups sugar
⅔ cup shortening
2 cups flour
½ tsp baking soda
½ tsp ground nutmeg

1 tsp ground cinnamon
½ tsp salt
2 eggs, beaten
4 cups sliced apples

½ cup nuts, chopped
½ cup butter
½ cup cream
½ cup brown sugar
1 tsp vanilla

Prep Time
30 min

Cooking Time
35 min

Serves
12

1. Preheat the oven at 350°F / 180°C.
2. Cream together sugar and shortening.
3. Sift together flour, baking soda, nutmeg, cinnamon and salt. Add to creamed mixture.
4. Add eggs, apples and nuts and mix well.
5. Transfer to a greased 9" x 13" pan.
6. Bake for 35 min or till toothpick comes out clean.
7. Mix butter, cream, sugar and vanilla. Bring to a boil for 1 ½ min and serve over cake.

Contributor: Ruth Des Cotes, Environmental Educator at Brooksdale

"This one came from a very old cookbook that I think Rob picked up from Salvation Army in his penniless days. I tried it and who wouldn't LOVE all those healthy apples - and maybe the sauce too!"

Mary-Ruth's Brownies

1 ½ cups flour
1 ½ - 2 cups sugar
½ cup and 2 tbs cocoa

1 tsp salt
1 cup oil
4 eggs

2 tsp vanilla
1 cup nuts (optional)

Prep Time
10 min

Cooking Time
30 min

Serves
12

1. Preheat the oven at 350°F / 180°C.
2. Beat all ingredients together for 3 min.
3. Transfer to a greased 9" x 13" pan.
4. Bake for 20-30 min or till toothpick comes out clean.

Contributors: Mary-Ruth and Loren Wilkinson, Friends of A Rocha Canada

I first learned how to make this from Alison Duncan, our first A Rocha Canada intern! Her mum helped cook at Pioneer Pacific camp for an Imago Dei retreat - how's that for connections!

It was a hit at first bite for me! Actually, at that retreat, Loren and Mary-Ruth Wilkinson were rowing the Kingfisher to come speak for us. The wind was blowing too briskly, and they were towed in to the camp by a merciful boater. So there are lots of relationship threads all tied together in one weekend!

Ruth Des Cotes

Baked Oatmeal

Dry
3 cups rolled oats
2 tsp baking powder
½ cup brown sugar

Wet
½ cup vegetable oil/ apple sauce
1 cup milk
1 egg

A variety of fresh/ dried fruits and nuts as desired, chopped (e.g. 1 cup raisins)

Prep Time
15 min

Cooking Time
40 min

Serves
5-6

1. Preheat the oven at 350°F / 180°C.
2. In a medium bowl, mix dry ingredients.
3. Beat together oil, milk and egg in another bowl. Add in a variety of chopped fruits and nuts.
4. Mix wet ingredients into dry ingredients.
5. Spread the mixture evenly onto a greased 8" x 8" pyrex dish.
6. Bake for 35-40 min.

TIP
Try with apples, raisins, apricots and cranberries!

Rick's Tip
Put the mixture into the fridge overnight, then pop it into the oven the next morning - just not a cold glass dish into a hot oven!

I made crêpes once at Brooksdale and I think "overwhelmed" would be the best word to describe the way I felt as I saw the crêpes disappear as soon as they arrived on the serving table. The worst part was that people, while waiting, started to eat the toppings by themselves!

I thought the timing would be all right, especially since I had help from at least four fellow interns, but even the last three hours of the afternoon were not enough.

So you can't underestimate the time it takes to prepare crêpes for 30 people or more. Apart from that, it was nice teaching anyone willing to learn how to make a crêpe and seeing some doing a far better job than me!"

David Nussbaumer

French Crêpes

5 eggs
4 cups flour
4 cups milk

3 tbs oil
½ cup beer

Prep Time
20 min

Cooking Time
2 h

Serves
10

Part 1

1. In a large bowl, add 2 cups of flour. Add eggs, one at a time, and mix well after adding each egg.

2. Add a bit of milk, mix well, then some flour and mix well. Repeat till you have added all the milk and flour.

3. Add the oil and the beer, and mix well. If your batter has lumps, run it through a sieve. (Well done if there are no lumps!)

4. Let it rest for 1 hour.

Part 2

5. When ready, put a non-stick frying pan over medium heat.

6. Using a small/medium ladle, add just enough of the crêpe batter so that it forms a thin layer inside the pan. When your crêpe is ready on one side (starting to get a bit brown), turn over.

7. Keep crêpes warm, either on a plate placed on top of a pot of boiled water or in an oven at a very low temperature.

SAVOURY
TOPPINGS
Ham, bacon, grated cheese, mushrooms, deep-fried zucchinis, etc.

SWEET
TOPPINGS
Peanut butter, honey, jam, maple syrup, sliced bananas, fresh berries, various nuts, almonds, whipped cream, chocolate sauce, lemon juice, ice cream, etc.

The second day of our Galiano working retreat consisted of collecting walnuts for drying, using a traditional press to make some wondrous apple cider and most importantly the rewarding task of confecting homemade ice cream.

To the task of ice cream making, five faithful workers were assigned. Their responsibility was to keep the crank turning and the ice topped up. As the ice cream slowly thickened and our muscles tired, our shifts at the crank grew shorter and shorter. The ice cream bucket needed more and more stabilizing as the ice cream stiffened, so we ended up taking turns sitting on its top in order to continue cranking.

Finally the task was completed, the top came off and our reward stared at us. We each got a spoon and tested it, a heavenly sweetness met our hungry taste buds. Creamy satisfaction!

Philip Baskin

Homemade Ice Cream
For a hand crank ice cream maker

6 cups raspberries or other fruits
Juice from 3 lemons
6 cups cream
6 cups milk
4 cups sugar
1 cup corn syrup
1 box of coarse salt
Crushed ice

Prep Time
10 min

Cranking Time
30 min

Serves
12

Variation
Use 2% milk for a lighter ice cream!

1. Blend thawed fruit and lemon juice in food processor.
2. In a bowl, mix together cream, milk, sugar and corn syrup.
3. Place canister into bucket, followed by "dasher" twin blades. Ensure dasher is centred on the peg and turns freely.
4. Pour cream mixture into canister and place lid onto canister. Again, ensure the dasher turns freely.
5. Secure and lock hand crank to canister and bucket.
6. Add crushed ice and salt in alternating layers. End with a top layer of salt. Note: Be generous with the salt.
7. Start cranking! As the ice melts, add more ice and salt as necessary.
8. Once the cream mixture starts to thicken, add the blended fruit and lemon juice.
9. Keep cranking till you can't do it anymore. Then, do it a bit more. :) The cranking should take about 30 min or so.

Always a highlight at the Galiano Working Retreat!

Contributor: Rick Faw, Vice-President of A Rocha Canada

Then an old man, a keeper of an inn, said, "Speak to us of Eating and Drinking." And he said: Would that you could live on the fragrance of the earth, and like an air plant be sustained by the light. But since you must kill to eat, and rob the young of its mother's milk to quench your thirst, let it then be an act of worship, And let your board stand an altar on which the pure and the innocent of forest and plain are sacrificed for that which is purer and still more innocent in man. When you kill a beast say to him in your heart, "By the same power that slays you, I too am slain; and I too shall be consumed. For the law that delivered you into my hand shall deliver me into a mightier hand. Your blood and my blood is naught but the sap that feeds the tree of heaven." And when you crush an apple with your teeth, say to it in your heart, "Your seeds shall live in my body, And the buds of your tomorrow shall blossom in my heart, And your fragrance shall be my breath, And together we shall rejoice through all the seasons." And in the autumn, when you gather the grapes of your vineyard for the winepress, say in your heart, "I too am a vineyard, and my fruit shall be gathered for the winepress, And like new wine I shall be kept in eternal vessels." And in winter, when you draw the wine, let there be in your heart a song for each cup; And let there be in the song a remembrance for the autumn days, and for the vineyard, and for the winepress.

Khalil Jibran, *The Prophet*

Welsh Cakes

I cup butter, softened
I cup sugar
I egg
I tbs lemon juice
3 cups flour

2 tsp baking powder
I tsp nutmeg
I cup currants or raisins

Prep Time
10 min

Cooking Time
30 min

Serves
12

1. Whisk butter and sugar till creamy.
2. Add the egg and lemon juice, and mix.
3. In a separate bowl, sift together flour, baking powder and nutmeg.
4. Add to the butter mixture and blend well. Stir in the currants/raisins.
5. Roll the dough on a floured surface and cut into rounds with a jar or glass.
6. Fry cake rounds on an ungreased frying pan over medium-low heat. Flip them when golden brown.

"During my summer as an intern, we went on a boat trip to Pender Island and different watches were responsible for different meals. I was part of Ruth's watch, and we decided to do Welsh Cakes for a snack one day.

I'd never had them before and they were delicious. We first ate them as a snack on the boat, and they became an iconic food for me that weekend. They represented all the fun and adventures we had on the boat trip."

Nicole Ensing, Summer 2011 Sustainable Agriculture/ Administration Intern at Brooksdale

Variation
The traditional shape is round but try with other shapes too!

You cause grass to grow for the livestock
and plants for people to use. You allow
them to produce food from the earth —
wine to make them glad, olive oil to soothe
their skin, and bread to give them strength.

Psalm 104: 14-15

This & That

I had never considered myself a "real French" until I came to A Rocha and discovered the massive cubic orange thing that North-Americans grate and put on top of casseroles and dare to call "cheese"!

That's why at the end of the summer, making the most of a ride to the US (where the merchandise is slightly cheaper), I bought a few cheese "species" and suggested having a tasting evening. The cheese was to be consumed with red wine and French style baguettes. I must admit that my experience in bread making at this point was... non-existent!

Although the shape and taste was a far cry from baguettes, I wasn't too disappointed. The Canadians remained faithful to their famous extreme politeness and were very encouraging. It was indeed an enjoyable night, which happened to coincide with the 40th birthday of our beloved centre director.

David Nussbaumer

Baguettes

4 cups bread flour

⅓ cups warm water

2 tsp baker's yeast

2 tsp salt

Prep Time
1h 15 min

Cooking Time
25 min

Serves
2 loaves

Part 1

1. In a large bowl, mix the flour and the salt. Create a large well and pour the dry yeast in the centre.
2. Add the warm water. Mix gently with the end of the fingers and progressively work the dough until it forms a nice ball.
3. Place the ball in a lightly-oiled bowl and cover with a dishcloth. Let rest for at least 30 min.

Part 2

4. Divide the dough in two smaller balls. Flatten and form a square shape. Fold the sides in order to get two thin rolls.
5. Form the points of the baguettes and let them rest for at least 40 min.

Part 3

6. Preheat the oven at 450-460°F / 240°C
7. When the dough has risen, incise the top to make it look like professional bread.
8. Put the baguettes in the oven and reduce temperature to 400°F / 200°C. Bake for 20-25 min until golden brown.

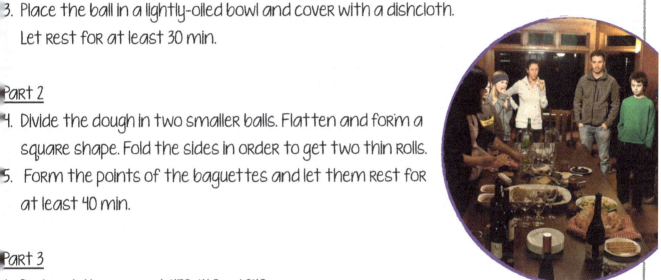

Cheese Accompaniments
Brie, Comté, Camembert, Gruyère, Goat's Cheese, Blue Cheese, etc.

Adapted from www.meilleurduchef.com

Contributor: David Nussbaumer, Summer 2013 Conservation Intern at Brooksdale

76

We eat plenty of bread. It is always a hit in our house — in fact, our six year old daughter is certain it is the only food she needs. Not only is it tasty to eat, it is also great to make.

But for some reason, yeast used to make me nervous, and I would avoid making yeast doughs! However, one recipe changed it all for me: I found a "No Knead Bread" recipe in a magazine. I tentatively tried it — and succeeded! So I tried it again. It worked a second time! It felt like I could not fail! So I tried it again, and again, and again.

Mostly, it worked: any baker will experience a bad batch once in a while. However, by simply observing what I was doing and how the dough responded, I learned — and enjoyed it!

Intriguingly, our six year old also enjoys making bread. She loves getting dough on her hands and scoring the top, making a pattern on the top of the bread as it rises and bakes.

Wes Smith

Basic No-knead Artisan Bread

3 cups lukewarm water
1 ½ tbs granulated yeast
1 ½ tbs coarse kosher or sea salt
6 ½ cups all-purpose flour, unsifted

Prep Time
4 h

Cooking Time
30 min

Serves
4 small loaves

Step 1

1. In a large bowl, add yeast to water. Stir to dissolve.
2. Add half of flour, then salt. Stir into a smooth batter.
3. Add rest of flour. Stir well or use wet hands to mix together till uniformly moist.
4. Cover and leave to rise for 2-4 h. If refrigerated, allow to warm up at room temperature 1-2 h before shaping.

Dough will keep up to 2 weeks in the refrigerator!

Step 2

5. When ready to bake, sprinkle flour on surface of dough and tear/cut off a chunk (1 lb of dough = grapefruit size). The recipes gives about 4 lbs of dough, enough for 4 small loaves.
6. Add more flour as needed to keep dough from sticking to your hands.
7. Shape a boule (round loaf) by gently stretching surface of dough around to the bottom, rotating a ¼ turn as you go. The result will be a "tight" ball and should take less than 30 sec. Alternatively, press 4 corners down to make bottom flat.
8. Place boule on a cornmeal dusted baking sheet or line baking sheet with parchment paper. Cover with plastic wrap and leave to rise for 40 min.

[Continued]

> "Baking is not hard! Anyone can do it, not just pros. YOU are the baker! Enjoy the process, and once you have confidence with the basics, experiment!"

Step 3

1. If you have a baking stone or tile, place on middle rack and preheat oven at 450°F / 230°C. Also insert a broiler tray on lower rack.
2. Dust flour on dough and make 1 cm deep cuts on top of dough.
3. Transfer dough to oven and quickly pour 1 cup hot water onto broiler tray.
4. For 1 lb loaf, bake for 30 min till crust is nicely browned. For large loaf, bake for 40-45 min.

TIP
How do you know if your bread is baked? Tap it - it should sound hollow!

Suggestions

- For a slower rise time, use cooler water or reduce amount of yeast. Recipe will work with as little as ½-1 tsp of yeast! For ½ tsp yeast, it will take 6-12 h to rise, and the second rise can take 2-3 times longer. This way, you can start preparing the dough in the evening, let it rise overnight and bake the next morning!
- Substitute 1-3 cups all-purpose flour with whole wheat flour, corn flour or rye flour.
- Add some dried herbs like dill, basil, rosemary, sage and oregano.
- Use this recipe for pizza crust.
- For foccacia bread, flatten dough to ½-¾ inch thick. Drizzle olive oil and sprinkle coarse salt and rosemary. Bake for 20 min, without broiler tray.
- For pita bread, make small rounds. Dust well with flour and roll flat. Bake on hot stone at 500-550°F / 260-290°C for 5-7 min.

Adapted from Artisan Bread in Five Minutes a Day: The Discovery That Revolutionizes Home Baki by Jeff Hertzberg and Zoe Francois and http://selfreliantcommunity.wordpress.com
Contributor: Paul Neufeld and Wes Smith, Farm Managers at Brooksdale

When our eating is informed by God's love and care, we participate in the new humanity made possible by Jesus Christ, who is called our true food and drink... Eating, we can now see, is one of the most fundamental ways we know for communicating our life together as a gift gratefully received and cherished.

Norman Wirzba, *Living the Sabbath*

... the more eaters who vote with their forks for a different kind of food, the more commonplace and accessible such foods will become.

Michael Pollan, *In Defense of Food*

Coconut & Maple Syrup Crunchy Granola

Dry
3 cups rolled oats
1 cup whole wheat flour
¾ cup brown sugar
1 ½ tsp ground cinnamon
½ tsp salt

Wet
¼ cup oil
¼ cup maple syrup
¼ cup coconut milk
1 ½ cups dried fruits, nuts and/or seeds

Prep Time
15 min

Cooking Time
40 min

Serves
10

1. Preheat the oven at 300°F / 150°C.

2. In a large bowl, mix the dry ingredients and make a well in the middle.

3. In another bowl, mix the wet ingredients.

4. Pour the wet mixture into the dry mixture well and mix thoroughly till all the loose flour has been incorporated.

5. Spread the mixture evenly onto two greased 9" x 13" pans.

6. Bake for 40 min, stirring well every 10 min till golden.

7. Leave to cool. Serve with organic milk, homemade yogurt and/or fresh seasonal fruits for a wholesome breakfast.

TIP
Baked granola turns crunchy after cooling down, not while baking.

"We ran out of milk one time, so Sandra and I experimented making Chunky Crunchy Granola (from Simply in Season) with coconut milk. It turned out to be a chewy, but really tasty "coconutty" granola! As we were still out of milk and honey the following week, I came up with an idea of using maple syrup - which tastes better and is also less sweet for a yummy breakfast COCONUT MAPLE SYRUP GRANOLA!"

adapted from Simply in Season

ontributor: Cheryl Man, Fall 2013 Conservation intern at Brooksdale

Together we began to understand all meals, and everything that went into the making of meals, as Eucharistic. The Holy Eucharist is a meal... prepared and served to God's people as they assemble at the Lord's table. The ultimate act of hospitality, the matrix of all hospitality. Everything and everyone is interconnected in an organic way... and all the meals we eat at home... are a derivative in some deep and powerful sense from the Lord's Supper. When we realized that all meals have a Eucharistic shape, all the motifs of worship began to get worked into the meals we ate in common around our tables in our homes and beyond —
Coming to the table where Christ is the host is hospitality at its most complete, receiving Christ and the entire Creation and community of Christ in thanksgiving.

Eugene Peterson, *The Pastor*

Eggnog

12 egg yolks
0.45 kg/1 lb icing sugar
2 cups dark rum
2-4 cups brandy✳

2 L whipping cream
8-12 egg whites
Ground nutmeg

Prep Time
2h + Overnight

Serves
4 litres

Part 1

1. Beat egg yolks till light in colour.
2. Gradually beat in sugar.
3. While beating constantly, add rum very slowly.
4. Cover mixture with a cloth and let it stand for 1 h.

Part 2

5. Add brandy and whipping cream, while beating constantly.
6. Cover and refrigerate overnight (or for at least 3 h).

Part 3

7. Beat egg whites till stiff. Fold lightly into mixture.
8. Sprinkle nutmeg and serve.

✳**Brandy**
2 cups for other ingredients to stand out, or 4 cups for a stronger alcohol taste!

Note
With the risk of salmonella from raw eggs, it is recommended that children, elderly and people with compromised immune systems refrain from eating raw eggs unless you use pasteurized eggs.

"This wonderfully rich, fortified drink was our office favourite holiday treat. It is nothing like the store-bought equal. A little will go a long way and only draw you into having more. This rich blend of cream, icing sugar and eggs masks the ample quantity of alcohol, so as little as a quarter cup is quite a lot. Enjoy!"

Pretty Good Cornbread

1 ½ cups cornmeal
2 ½ cups milk
2 cups all-purpose flour
1 tbs baking powder

1 tsp salt
Up to ⅔ cup white sugar
2 eggs
½ cup vegetable oil

Prep Tim
30 mi

Cooking T
1 h

Serves
1 loat

1. Preheat the oven at 400°F / 200°C.
2. In a medium bowl, combine cornmeal and milk. Leave to soak for 5 min.
2. In a large bowl, combine dry ingredients and then add cornmeal mixture.
3. Beat eggs and oil together, then add to the mixture. Mix till smooth.
3. Pour batter into a greased 9" x 13" baking pan.
4. Bake for 30-35 min or till skewer comes out clean.
5. Slice, serve with honey butter* and enjoy!

TIP
When mixing ingredients, less is more. Your cornbread will rise beautifully if you don't beat every little lump out of it.

*To make honey butter, simply soften butter and mix with honey and spread on top of your cornbread.

Contributor: Emily Upcott, 2013 Conservation Intern at Brooksdale

Pumpkin, Maple & Pecan Loaf

Dry

1 ½ cups gluten-free, all-purpose flour
1 ¾ tsp ground cinnamon
½ tsp ground nutmeg
½ tsp ground ginger

¼ tsp ground allspice
⅛ tsp ground cloves
¼ tsp sea salt
1 tsp baking powder
¾ cup pecans, chopped

Wet

½ cup butter, softened
2 large eggs
1 cup pure maple syrup ✱

1 tbs vanilla extract
1 ⅓ cups pumpkin puree

Prep Time
15 min

Cooking Time
1h 5 min

Serves
1 loaf

1. Preheat the oven at 350°F / 180°C.
2. Lightly grease loaf pan with butter or cooking spray.
3. In a large bowl, cream together the wet ingredients.
4. In a medium bowl, combine dry ingredients.
5. Fold dry ingredients into large bowl, combining till just moistened.
6. Transfer to a lightly greased 5" x 10" loaf pan.
7. Bake for 60-65 min or till skewer comes out clean.
8. Cool for 10 min before transferring to wire rack.

✱ WHAT MAKES GRADE B MAPLE SYRUP SO NUTRITIOUS?
Grade B Syrup is dark and usually thicker. The reason for its appearance is the different concentrations of sugars present both early and later in the season. Sap from the start of the season produces the palest syrup, while the later season creates the darkest and richest syrup.

Organic Grade B Maple Syrup also does not go through the same refinement process as commercial grade maple syrups. This artificial process strips many of the natural, essential nutrients out of it, as well as unnecessarily adding extra sugar and chemicals.

[From www.gradebmaplesyrup.org]

These quinoa pancakes were a class-pleaser at one of the Girls in Action sessions designed to equip elementary school age girls at risk with confidence and new skills through activities on healthy living and environmental stewardship.

We brought a healthy snack for them each week, and when it was my turn to make one, pancakes seemed to be the most obvious satisfying choice. Some of my favourite memories involving food are those in which I either experienced a friend's care by sitting down to a surprise pancake breakfast, or I was the one wielding the spatula in my own act of care. These fluffy little circles of unpretentious goodness somehow signalled that it's okay to let your guard down. It's okay to feel comfortable around your fellow sticky eaters who were attempting to decorate their pancakes with drizzles of syrup.

Making snacks for the Girls In Action group was a privilege. It's funny how the mere act of bringing food to the school imparted a sense of hospitality, even though we weren't hosting the students at the centre. In essence, we invited the girls to share in our community and all the things we value, while caring for their physical well-being in a tangible way.

Sandra Dumitras

Quinoa Pancakes

cup quinoa, cooked
¾ cup all-purpose flour
2 tsp baking powder
½ tsp salt

2 large eggs
1 tbs unsalted butter, melted or vegetable oil
¼ cup low-fat milk
2 tbs pure honey

Prep Time
10 min

Cooking Time
20 min

Serves
5

1. In a medium bowl, whisk together quinoa, flour, baking powder and salt.

2. In another medium bowl, whisk together eggs, butter, milk and honey until smooth.

3. Add egg mixture to flour mixture. Whisk to combine.

4. Lightly coat a large nonstick skillet or griddle with butter and heat over medium-high. Drop batter by heaping tablespoonfuls into skillet. Cook until bubbles appear on top, about 2 min. Flip cakes and cook until golden brown on underside, about 2 min.

5. Wipe skillet clean and repeat (reduce heat to medium if over-browning).

6. Serve with honey and fresh fruit if desired.

Quinoa contributes an unexpected, nutty taste and crunchy texture!

No community can rest in its present level of hospitality towards others. All our actions towards others can be tested by whether they are in harmony with whole hearted feasting together eventually.

David F. Ford, *The Shape of Living*

Savoury Zucchini Bread

3 cups flour
4 tsp baking powder
½ tsp baking soda
1 tsp salt
1 cup zucchini, coarsely shredded
¾ cup sharp cheese, shredded
¼ cup scallions/chives, chopped

3 tbs fresh parsley, chopped
1 tbs fresh dill, snipped or 2 tsp dried
2 large eggs
1 cup buttermilk
¼ cup warm melted butter

Prep Time
30 min

Cooking Time
1 h

Serves
1 loaf

1. Preheat the oven at 300°F / 150°C.
2. In a large bowl, whisk together flour, baking powder, baking soda and salt.
3. Add zucchini, cheese, scallions, parsley and dill. Toss to coat with flour.
4. In another bowl, whisk together eggs, buttermilk and butter.
5. Add to flour mixture, and mix lightly till dry ingredients are moistened. (Avoid over-mixing or the batter will be lumpy.)
6. Transfer to a greased loaf tin.
7. Bake for 55-60 min or till skewer comes out clean.

TIP
Cool on a
rack for a few
minutes before
removing to cool
completely!

"I love this because it uses plentiful garden vegetables, and makes a delicious quick bread - adding cheese just makes it more irresistible!

This recipe was featured in the CSA newsletter, the first year we got a CSA share (helpfully dated, 2005). The whole family loved it! Thank you, Paul."

Honey, Lemon & Barley Drink

1 cup barley
6 cups water

3 tbs honey
Fresh lemon juice and zest

Total Tim
30 mi

Serves
4

1. Rinse barley in cold water till water runs clear.
2. In a medium pot, boil barley, lemon zest and water on high heat, with tilted lid. Reduce heat and simmer at least 20 min.
3. Strain barley water into a heatproof bowl.
   Optional: return some barley back into water.
4. Add honey and lemon juice and adjust as desired.
5. Serve warm or refrigerate for cool drink.

Barley
is a rich source
of fibre, vitamins B
and E and minerals
like calcium and
iron.

Contributor: Pamela Soo, Fall 2013 Environmental Education Intern at Brooksdale

Homemade Flu-Fighting Tea

Total Tim
15 min

Serves
3

3 cups water
1 cinnamon stick
3 slices fresh ginger
1 tbs dried red dates
¼ tsp cloves

½ tbs turmeric
1 pinch cayenne
1 ½ tbs raw honey
Juice of half a lemon

For a quick easy version, boil ginger and red dates for 10 min and serve with honey.

1. In a pot, add all ingredients except honey and lemon juice. Bring to a boil, then reduce heat and simmer for 10 min.
2. Place honey and lemon juice in a mug.
3. Strain tea and serve warm.

Vitamin-
packed red
dates help to
boost immunity
and adds a lovely
sweetness to
the tea.

Adapted from http://www.chatelaine.com/health/wellness/flu-fighting-tea/

Contributor: Shai Kroeker, 2011 Environmental Education Intern at Brooksdale

Perhaps The World Ends Here
By Joy Harjo

The world begins at a kitchen table.
No matter what, we must eat to live.

The gifts of earth are brought and prepared, set on the table.
So it has been since creation, and it will go on.

We chase chickens or dogs away from it.
Babies teethe at the corners. They scrape their knees under it.

It is here that children are given instructions on what it means
to be human. We make men at it, we make women.

At this table we gossip, recall enemies and the ghosts of lovers.

Our dreams drink coffee with us as they put their arms around our
children. They laugh with us at our poor falling-down selves and as
we put ourselves back together once again at the table.

This table has been a house in the rain, an umbrella in the sun.

Wars have begun and ended at this table. It is a place to hide in
the shadow of terror. A place to celebrate the terrible victory.

We have given birth on this table,
and have prepared our parents for burial here.

At this table we sing with joy, with sorrow.
We pray of suffering and remorse. We give thanks.

Perhaps the world will end at the kitchen table, while we are
laughing and crying, eating of the last sweet bite.

Making Healthy Food Choices

We may from time to time wonder what and how we should be eating. Who do you listen to when creating your family's dinner menu? There are a myriad of voices clamouring for our culinary attention. Many of these voices are supposed "experts" — from doctors and diet books to government advisory commissions and food pyramids to the health claims on food packages themselves. What is needed amidst all the clamour is a clarion voice, one who can speak with simplicity and no nonsense wisdom.

Here at A Rocha, we have found Michael Pollan's slim volume *Food Rules* to be this clarion voice. It is chock full of pithy and even proverbial "rules" to live and eat by. At the top of the list is:

> *"Eat food. Not too much. Mostly plants."*

This is the bottom line — a piece of hard ground, deep down at the bottom of the swamp of nutrition science — seven words of plain English, no biochemistry degree required. The wisdom of Pollan's advice can be clearly seen in the statistics, which show that generally people eating a wide range of traditional diets consisting primarily of vegetables, fruits, and whole grains have a lower rate of many chronic diseases such as obesity, Type 2 diabetes, cardiovascular disease and cancer than those whose diets consist mainly of highly processed foods and meat.

Starting a healthy food journey

The first task when embarking on a food journey that is good for you and good for the planet is to distinguish real foods - the plants, animals, and fungi people have been eating for generations - from the highly processed products of modern food science. Each of Pollan's rules serves as a filter for separating the one from the other, and they all share a common aim — to help keep the unhealthy stuff out of your shopping cart. Consider the following list from *Food Rules*:

- Do not eat anything your great-grandmother wouldn't recognize as food.
- Avoid food products containing ingredients that a third-grader cannot pronounce.
- Shop the peripheries of the supermarket and stay out of the middle.
- Eat only foods that will eventually rot.
- Eat only foods that have been cooked by humans.
- Do not ingest foods made in places where everyone is required to wear a surgical cap.
- If it came from a plant, eat it; if it was made in a plant, don't.
- It is not food if it arrived through the window of your car.

What *sorts* of food should I eat?

We firmly believe that it is possible to nourish ourselves from an astonishing range of foods. There have been, and can be, healthy high-fat and healthy low-fat diets, both built around whole foods. Yet there are some whole foods that are better for us than others, and some ways of producing and combining them in meals that can make a difference. Pollan's rules in this section propose a handful of personal principles regarding what to eat.

- Eat mostly plants, especially leaves.
- Treat meat as a flavouring or special occasion food.
- Eat animals that have themselves eaten well.
- Eat well-grown food from healthy soil.
- Do not overlook the oily little fishes.
- Eat some foods that have been pre-digested by bacteria or fungi (fermentation).
- Sweeten and salt your food yourself.
- Eat all the junk food you want as long as you cook it yourself.

How and how much should I eat?

Apart from addressing the question of what to eat in the previous two sections, this section deals with something a bit more elusive but no less important: the set of manners, eating habits, taboos, and unspoken guidelines that together govern a person's (and a culture's) relationship to food and eating. *How* you eat may have as much bearing on your health (and your weight) as *what* you eat. Michael Pollan's food rules in this section are designed to foster a healthier relationship to food, whatever you're eating.

- Stop eating before you are full.
- Eat when you are hungry, not when you are bored.
- Eat slowly.
- Eat "Breakfast like a king, lunch like a prince, dinner like a pauper."
- Eat meals.
- Do not get your fuel from the same place your car does.
- Do all your eating at a table. No, a desk is not a table.
- Cook.

Taken as a whole, these simple rules can guide us out of the fog of pseudo-scientific food like substances and ground us firmly back in the land of milk and honey.

"Taste and See that the LORD is good!"
A Collection of Reflections on Food and Faith

1. Reflection by Farmer Wes Smith

I enjoy improving old systems. Sometimes this means re-working the old system, but other times it entails creating an entirely new one. This has been true of different parts of my life, but as a farmer, this has helped me time and time again.

There are many elements to be considered in planning a garden. The soil and its history are considered. The climate and weather patterns and reviewed. Then we think about what people will eat, taking special note of those vegetables to which we are culturally endeared, ensuring we plant these. But we also plant new discoveries — those vegetables that we do not know how to eat but are edible and would grow well in our garden's environment, providing nutrients. Furthermore, when planning a garden, we are mindful of how different vegetables store into the winter and spring, mindfully engaging in a food system that encourages local and seasonal. We want to make the most of our time and efforts, and the only way to do this is to spend time considering these elements.

At Brooksdale, the relationship of community to the many parts of life is always a part of the conversation. This is true of our relationship with the garden. The produce is not the result of one individual's efforts; we require the help and efforts of many to experience success in growing. The vegetables we grow are the result of the community's work. Of course, not all in the A Rocha community have logged hours in the garden in order to receive their portion. No! Being a part of the community is growing for the benefit of the whole!

When the thoughts and efforts that contribute to garden production are considered, it acts as a catalyst for the community to constructively engage in conversation about how to better grow, better eat, and better live together.

2. Reflection by Farmer Katie Wood

As an amateur gardener, canning enthusiast and locovoire wannabe, I came to Brooksdale with the hopes of really experiencing eating seasonally, with no "out" to run to the grocery store for all my food whims. I was really excited to take my idealistic plans to a whole new level by participating in a community that ate only what they grew, and made socially responsible purchases for the items that could not be grown at Brooksdale. I was, after all, signed up for a Sustainable Agriculture internship, and was going to learn how to live off the land! So it came as a mighty big shock to me to see a bowl of bananas and oranges in our wee kitchen at the Coach House on my first day. I quickly learned that we were not able to live the way I had imagined. Although I was disappointed, I was partly relieved because being asked to cook meals for 10–30 people was a scary thing for me, and I had to rely heavily on recipes. Using recipes instead of culinary creativity is not a good survival tactic for someone wanting to only eat locally. You cannot always find a recipe featuring rutabaga and leeks at your fingertips! The staff encouraged substitutions (use kale buds instead of broccoli, tah-tsai instead of spinach) which was nice, but as a cook with little confidence, it was just a little too risky for my comfort level to test out on a new crowd.

As winter turned to spring and I learned more about the food available, it became easier to rely on the garden to provide all the veggies for our meals. Cooking for large groups became less daunting, and I was able to experiment a lot more. By summertime, we were eating our veggies solely from the garden. I was in awe of the abundance that came from one small seed. The garden truly is a beautiful and bountiful place. We worked hard to communicate what was available to help people to plan for cooking, but it wasn't always easy. In fact, it was sometimes frustrating! I would become critical if people didn't use the vegetables that were exploding out of our harvest bins and filling the fridges until the doors wouldn't close. I could not see the bigger picture. What I should have understood all along was that A Rocha is a community of people from a different backgrounds, filled with different passions, talents, and ideas, who come together out of their love for God and God's Creation, and who express that love in all sorts of ways. A fellow intern helped me see that I was viewing it all wrong. I had come expecting to find legalism and limitation around food, and wanted to have an "experience", but what I received was much richer than that.

Anyone coming to A Rocha with the same ambitions as I had should proceed cautiously, because it's easy for those goals to turn selfish and prideful. It's like anything in life - with no love, and no room for sharing, changing, and growing, you miss the whole point of living in community as the body of Christ. With a little help (okay, a lot of help) from fellow interns and Brooksdale staff, I came to appreciate that everyone brings something special to our table, and along the way, we all find out for ourselves what it means to eat responsibly, mindfully, and seasonally, with a sense of gratitude to our Creator for the gift of daily bread....or if you are here in July, the gift of daily zucchini!

3. Reflection by Anna Baird (2010 Spring - Summer Intern)

I think we'd been at the centre less than 48 hours, still groggy from our 24h journey from New Zealand, when we watched the documentary *King Corn* about industrialised agriculture in North America and its damaging effects on the land, the animals, the farmers, and the consumers. This was a huge eye-opener and the beginning of a completely new way of looking at food and faith. The intentionality at A Rocha Canada around all things to do with food has shaped us in surprising ways. We've come to see that loving our neighbour involves loving the cow and the chicken that provide for us, loving the earth that sustains them, loving the coffee grower in Ghana, as well as loving the guest that joins us for a meal.

To begin with, I would duck out at weekends to the shops to stave off my craving for meat and sugar, and I would despair at having to cook lunch for 30 people with seemingly only dried beans and more kale from the garden to work with. But by the end of our six months' stay, we'd learned to make yogurt, pasta, bread, and pesto, learned to cook for 80 people, learned to eat what was in season, personally killed and eaten resident roosters, and fallen in love with this lifestyle that demonstrates God's desire for shalom for all parts of Creation.

Back at home, we continue on this journey of learning to eat well. We eat less meat, more homegrown vegetables, we pay three times the price of ordinary sugar for the privilege of supporting fair trade for cane sugar growers abroad. We try to avoid buying what we could make ourselves and we're grateful to be able to keep chickens and grow vegetables. We also value hospitality and community living more than ever, and are now living in community here back at home, sharing our meals and our lives together with half a dozen others and their children. I encourage you to throw yourself into life at the centre, learn as much as you can, get your hands dirty in the garden and the kitchen and be open to being challenged and transformed. You won't regret it.

4. Reflection by Shai Kroeker (2011 Intern)

My one year internship at Brooksdale enriched me deeply about food, grace and hospitality. I also rediscovered my love for cooking and the joy of making food! With a weekly cooking duty for lunch or dinner, where on average there were 25 people eating per meal, I was very excited to cook in a brand new kitchen where there is lots of space and full kitchen equipment. I felt I was in a kitchen wonderland! I soon realized that cooking for a crowd was a daunting task and my cooking enthusiasm was challenged by the lack of the ingredients I wanted. I have come to appreciate the beautiful rhythmic pattern of growing vegetables seasonally in the garden and the glorious flavours each of these vegetables develop until they are ready for harvest. I say this because I never liked eating certain raw veggies like carrots and broccoli back home in Singapore. But being here and having the chance to eat the freshest carrot or broccoli straight from the soil, I realised how sweet they taste! Even bok choy and Chinese cabbage taste so sweet on its own! As a Chinese, I have never eaten the latter two veggies raw but my experience at A Rocha has taught me that when we honour the stewardship of the environment God has given us — by caring for the land, water, air and everything in it — we will enjoy God's bountiful blessing of splendid foods! It is actually quite fun to learn how to choose suitable vegetables to cook a particular meal. My knowledge of local vegetables has expanded to include celeriac, fairy pumpkin, kale, rutabaga, Swiss chard (a superfood!) and even foreign ones such as mizuna and Hungarian chillies. Eating less meat became a conscious choice and I learned to celebrate the humble beans and lentils that provide the necessary protein.

I always feel happy to be able to go to the garden, harvest the ingredients for making meals and bring them straight to the kitchen. The process of making lovely meals is my way of communing with God. I am thankful for His grace and I marvel at how He creates all these varieties of vegetables, meat and even the spices; each has its own distinctive taste or aroma and when you put them together, magically they are transformed into a meal that enlivens our senses, nourishes our body and deepens our appreciation of eating well. Grace is regularly practised by the community by being encouraging to the chef (no matter what is cooked!) and if the clock ticks past the designated meal time, they wait patiently for the meal to be served. I know this firsthand because when I was cooking, I was punctual only twice in the whole year!

I have put on new biblical lenses that Jesus' act of hospitality throughout the Bible is an act for me and all believers to follow. I didn't make that explicit connection to my faith before. Jesus was being hospitable to everyone he met and when he had to feed the 5000 in Matthew 14:13-21, he did so out of love and compassion. No one went away hungry and everyone was welcomed. Similarly at the dining table here at Brooksdale, loving and compassionate hospitality is extended to everyone who would like to join us as we partake in good food together, or just having a good cup of coffee or tea, with joyful thanksgiving and praise!

5. Reflection by Helen Yip (2011 Fall - 2012 Spring Intern)

"For where two or three gather in my name, there am I with them." (Matthew 18:20 NIV)

Food. It's as much of an experience and journey as it is a necessity. In September of 2011, I became a conservation science intern, moving onto the A Rocha Brooksdale Centre all the way from Edmonton, Alberta. Unknowingly, I stepped into a community that embraces eating and communing over the meal table with as much enthusiasm and intentionality (sometimes even more) as with the work they set out to do over the course of the day. During my experience at A Rocha, it dawned on me that meal times were sacred. My attitude towards meal times transformed from mere sustenance to appreciation and gratitude. I remember being in charge of cooking Tuesday lunches. That was my day. I would spend the rest of the week thinking about what to make and what we needed to use up from the cellars, or what I could harvest from the garden (in the Fall and even into the winter!). Cooking became a challenge and I like challenges.

I saw Farmer Paul and the interns spend countless hours in the garden, harvesting, or preparing the land for the upcoming growing season. These were man-hours that did not go unnoticed to my eyes. Realizing the care and attention that was needed in the garden, I tried to incorporate as much of what was produced in our garden into my meals. But like every newly graduated student that survived either off of their parent's leftovers, Kraft Dinner, or take out; beets, celeriac, turnips, purple carrots, kale and Brussels sprouts were not familiar ingredients. This is where cooking became a challenging but fun experience. It was about experimenting (like a good scientist) with these foreign ingredients, and hoping for the best that they would turn out delicious...or that there would be enough to go around. It was about understanding where the food came from and understanding the sacrifices that go behind it, be it man-hours, a life of a cow, or the amount of water, sunlight and nutrients that's needed to sustain such a living being, both plant and animal alike. The experience doesn't end there. When the food is served, something sacred happens. People put their work down and they flock. They flock from all directions and commune over the meal table. And trust me, I know Jesus is sitting there with us every time because the love that overflows from being in each other's company, and the love poured out from the food that was grown, harvested and prepared, is overwhelming. There's something to be said about food, in preparation and in consuming, whereby it becomes a part of us. Jesus exemplified that by breaking bread, and pouring wine. So let us come to the table with open hands, open hearts and open mouths.

Bon appétit.

6. Reflection by Matt Humphrey
Assistant Director, Brooksdale Centre

Jesus said, "This is what the kingdom of God is like. A man scatters seed on the ground. Night and day, whether he sleeps or gets up, the seed sprouts and grows, though he does not know how. All by itself the soil produces grain—first the stalk, then the head, then the full kernel in the head. As soon as the grain is ripe, he puts the sickle to it, because the harvest has come." (Mark 4: 26-29, NIV)

The Cambridge professor and former Dean of St. Paul's Cathedral, William Ralph Inge, once wrote, "The whole of nature is a conjugation of the verb 'to eat', in the active and passive." This is basic to the ecology of our world. All creatures must eat in order to live – we must take the life of other creatures, transforming their death into the blessing of life and sustenance for their bodies. Food remains one of the four central 'needs' that all creatures require: air, food, water, shelter. Children learn this in primary school, though seldom do adults give this much thought: our lives are utterly dependent on these gifts of Creation. If we fail to eat, we will surely perish. This is a basic need we share with all creatures.

Yet human eating transcends survival. It is not principally about survival that humans have developed thousands of cheeses, for example. Nor would creatures interested in survival alone spend several hours at elaborate coffee and wine tasting seminars. Beyond the sheer pleasure that eating brings us, we also have the remarkable gift of serving one another meals. All creatures eat food, but only humans, it would seem, have meals.

Along these lines, another Englishman, W. H. Auden, wrote, "The slogan of Hell: *Eat or be eaten.* The slogan of Heaven: *Eat and be eaten.*" Auden alerts us to the not-so-obvious fact that while all creatures *eat*, the fundamental orientation of that eating makes some deal of difference. It can be a sort of hell to live in a dog-eat-dog world, where survival is paramount: you must eat or be eaten. (Interesting to note in passing how this language of survival has been imported into our economic life.) But Auden holds out the possibility of another way, and in doing so is consistent with the biblical writers.

The psalmist declares, "How many are your works, Lord! In wisdom you made them all; the earth is full of your creatures." (104:24) An essential part of that wisdom, the psalmist adds, is the provision of food. "All creatures look to you to give them their food at the proper time. When you give it to them, they gather it up; when you open your hand, they are satisfied with good things." (104:27-28)

So we come to the dinner table the same way we come to the LORD's table – with open hands. Ready to receive that which will sustain our bodies as a sheer gift, recognizing with the eyes of faith that the simple soup before us is the gift of God for us and for all people – these gifts are meant to be shared! And we remember that these gifts, while transformed by our efforts, are nonetheless that – gifts, from a loving and generous Creator. As we 'take and eat', may we remember it is indeed God who feeds us, even as we will come to cook for and feed one another.

7. "Come and have breakfast" But don't forget your napkin!
by Mary-Ruth Wilkinson
Retired Regent College Professor and Friend of A Rocha

I am, until they kick me off, on the Altar Guild for our little Anglican church on Galiano Island—St. Margaret's of Scotland. Last week I had another try at getting the Eucharist "table setting" done properly—which is no small feat. Despite my "first-child" perfectionism, what I do never quite comes up to snuff. Last week it was the napkins. There are four of them: the "corporal", the "purificator", the "lavabo", and the all-purpose general napkin (I forget its name). I got the corporal fixed wrongly.

Ritual is very important in the Altar Guild tradition of setting the Table for the Eucharist. This meal is the meal of all meals. The significance of what goes on in this "Lord's Supper" is central to our faith. And thus, the way the "Lord's Table" is set is a way of affirming the crucial importance of this meal. For, in that "Last Supper" that the disciples shared with Jesus, their *Rabbouni*, their teacher, AND in our church communion meals we *re-member* the crux event of our faith—a moment that explodes with meaning—for all of us as Christians, certainly, but for us as human beings as well: "This is my body; This is my blood". Here, at the Lord's Table, we give thanks (*Eucharist* means "thanksgiving", with roots of gratitude and grace) to God for the love, grace, forgiveness, companionship (*com panis*—with bread) he shows us so abundantly in Jesus.

That last, before-death supper hallows all the meals we eat. All meals are a chance for us to choose: Will we be animals guzzling down fodder? Or humans graciously and gratefully thanking God for those gifts of creation which feed and nourish us?

Another meal with Jesus, the Breakfast at the Beach in John 21, gives us a "taste" of the "more than" physical "feeding" that meals can and should be. Here Jesus is the cook and host—he's built the fire and made a meal and serves it to the hungry seven fishermen who've slaved all night on the sea of Galilee with no fish to show for it. After filling their nets—giving them the chance to add to the meal (a truly equitable relationship!—companions in creation of the meal), he says, "Come and have breakfast". Then he opens up a conversation with Peter that is not only deeply forgiving (given Peter's three-times denial), but also richly affirming; he honours Peter with a job: "Feed my Sheep". These hungry seven were *fed* in every way: financially (all those 153 fish), bodily, psychologically, and spiritually. Most of all, they knew *him* as their true companion, and as their God: "It is the Lord!"

Well, you say, how do napkins play into all this? Margaret Visser, in her book *The Rituals of Dinner* claims (and shows), "As a meal the Mass spans all the meaning of eating at once. . . .all this and more is contained, expressed, and controlled by ritual"—including napkins (page 45).

Many rituals subtly undergird our meals — roundy-tipped knives, chewing with our mouths closed, passing serving bowls to each other, saying "grace", and hallowing our meals with candles (and napkins). Every meal, whether part of an Anglican Eucharist or a family breakfast, can be a way of saying, "I am a human being, created and loved by God, blessed with his gifts of daily bread — and I am thankful".

So, folks — all who are hungry for food and forgiveness, rest and restoration, comfort and companionship: "Come and have breakfast"! But don't forget your napkin!

Editor's Note

An education intern and a cookbook project?!

I'd never have imagined such a pairing myself before my internship with A Rocha Canada, but God definitely has a sense of humour! Among the array of environmental education projects Rick shared with us, the cookbook idea seemed like a fish out of water.

With my background work experience in environmental education, I was keen to help with the education resource gaps, yet eventually the cookbook was the one I felt most drawn to!

This labour of love has been my main project through most of the Fall 2013 term, which is why you might have noticed squash featuring rather prominently throughout the cookbook.

My hope is that you'll be richly blessed and inspired both by the joy of preparing food *for* and creating stories *with* those gathered at your table, as I have been here at Brooksdale.

Much love, Pamela

A Heartfelt Thank You!

To my wonderful supervisors, Rick & Ruth for the wisdom, guidance, encouragement and laughter shared throughout this term.

To all who took the time and effort to share your food recipes and stories - your input has made this cookbook possible.

Photography Credits

Many thanks to these people for contributing beautiful food & people photographs: Brooke McAllister, Cheryl Man, Christina Chan, David Nussbaumer, Katie Wood, Melissa Ong, Pamela Soo, Shai Kroeker, Zoe Matties and the A Rocha Canada photo gallery.

Credits for online photo resources:

Basic Stock http://daniellelevynutrition.com/2012/09/14/seasonal-september-soups/

Beet Borscht http://www.simplyrecipes.com/recipes/borscht/

French Crêpes French Crêpes http://www.stephmodo.com/2013/09/authentic-french-crepes.html

Granola http://www.abeautifulmess.com/2012/08/homemade-granola-3-ways.html

Honey Mustard Dressing http://www.mommypotamus.com/honey-mustard-dressing-recipe-5-minutes/

No-knead Bread http://www.notderbypie.com/snowed-in-means-no-knead-bread/

Palak Paneer http://www.vegrecipesofindia.com/palak-paneer/

Pumpkin Lasagna http://main.kitchendaily.com/recipe/easy-pumpkin-lasagna-151362/

Sesame Soba http://damndelicious.net/2013/06/17/sesame-soba-noodles/

Welsh Cakes http://hicookery.com/2011/03/01/welsh-cakes/

Vegetarian Pad Thai http://littleleopardbook.com/2013/01/22/whats-for-dinner-spicy-vegetable-pad-thai/

Grace
By Robert Farrar Capon

O Lord, refresh our sensibilities.
Give us this day our daily taste.

Restore to us soups that spoons will not sink in,
and sauces which are never the same twice.
Raise up among us stews with more gravy than we have to blot it with,
and casseroles that put starch and substance into our limp modernity.

Take away our fear of fat,
and make us glad of the oil which ran upon Aaron's beard.
Give us pasta with a hundred fillings,
and rice in a thousand variations.

Above all, give us grace to live as true men and women
- to fast till we come to a refreshed sense of what we have
and then to dine gratefully on all that comes to hand.

Drive far from us, O Most Bountiful,
all creatures of air and darkness; cast out the demons that possess us;
deliver us from the fear of calories and the bond of nutrition;
and set us free once more in our own land,
where we shall serve thee as thou hast blessed us
- with the dew of heaven,
the fatness of the earth, and plenty of corn and wine.

Amen.

Index

Numbers In The Kitchen

Approximate conversions between Imperial and Metric

VOLUME

1 teaspoon = 5 ml

1 tablespoon = 15 ml

¼ cup = 60 ml

⅓ cup = 80 ml

½ cup = 120 ml

1 cup = 240 ml

WEIGHT

1 oz = 30 grams

4 oz = ¼ lb = 115 grams

8 oz = ½ lb = 225 grams

16 oz = 1 lb = 455 grams

OVEN

150°F / 65°C

200°F / 90°C

250°F / 120°C

300°F / 150°C

350°F / 180°C

400°F / 200°C

DRIED TO COOKED

1 cup dried beans = 2 ½ cups cooked beans

1 cup dried quinoa = 1 ¼ cups cooked quinoa

1 cup dried lentils/chickpeas = 3 cups cooked lentils/chickpeas

1 cup dried white rice : 2 cups water

Doxology

♫

Praise God, from whom all blessings flow;
Praise Him, all creatures here below;
Praise Him above, ye heavenly host;
Praise Father, Son and Holy Ghost.
Amen.

Printed in the USA
CPSIA information can be obtained
at www.ICGtesting.com
LVHW060041121223
766265LV00060B/2516

9 780994 095602